Praise

Michael Brainard was instrumental in helping me hone my leadership skills and shape the contours of our corporate culture. With this book, *How to Become an Effective Leader*, he brings those impactful lessons to you. The disciplines he explains here will make you an even better version of yourself and make your mark with the work you do.

Gregory T. Lucier | Executive Chairman, CorzaHealth

Foundational reading for aspiring leaders and leaders aspiring to be great! What makes this book exceptional is the crisp distillation of leadership disciplines with a practical guide to implementation. No gimmicks.

Will Geist | Biotech Enterprise Leader

As a colleague, client, and active student of Michael's teachings over the past decade, I found *How to Become an Effective Leader* a clear, intuitive summation of his proven principles. I've seen first-hand how essential these eight disciplines can be to personal growth and in fostering a stable and self-sustaining organization. I wish I'd had access to this book when starting my career but look forward to making it a featured read within our internal leadership development programs.

Stephanie Goddard | CEO, Glidewell Dental

As we experience seismic shifts in workforce expectations for healthy work habits and more intentional leaders, Michael Brainard's actionable research and wisdom is the highest-value currency. In his crisp but powerful book, Michael covers the biology, biases, burdens, and behavioral building-blocks of compelling leadership.

Doug Holte | Founder, AWI

Michael is a no-nonsense leader that developed a highly effective process to distill the generic concept of leadership into actionable and relatable steps. *How to Become an Effective Leader* will challenge your assumptions about what it takes to be a great leader. After years of working with Michael and sending my entire executive team through his leadership training, I can attest that being a "deliberate and intentional" leader drives results. The characteristics that got you to where you are in your career aren't the same as those that are going to make you successful in your current role. Check your ego at the door and get ready for a great read.

Nate Johnson | President,
Lyon Living Development Company

I wanted to thank Michael for his continued contribution to our organization, executive development and personally for being my coach. This book provides wonderful insight into the impact of proper executive mindset, staff development, coaching and the disciplines required to be an effective leader. I am proud to call him a friend and grateful for his mentorship and guidance.

Mark Fuller | Chief Executive Officer,
LEED AP and Howard Building Corp

All leaders deal with the triple constraints of time, money, and resources. These constraints force us to make tradeoffs. So if you have to make a trade off on investing in one of your leadership strengths versus one of your leadership weaknesses, which do you pick? Have you identified the right one that will drive the greatest return on your time and money? Michael lays out a very concise way for all leaders at any level of an organization to assess their strengths and weaknesses as a leader and offers the reader the first few steps to improving performance on the never-ending journey that is leadership development.

Ken Ruggiero | Serial entrepreneur and Chairman of Goal Solutions, Goal Investment Management, and Ascent Funding

Michael distills countless careers and robust research into structured approaches to real leadership challenges. As a young executive and client, I've accelerated my knowledge and wisdom beyond my years thanks Michael. *How to Become an Effective Leader* goes beyond telling you how leaders become successful; it shows you how to develop strategies, turn them into tactics, and convert tactics into the ever-changing art of leadership.

Rodrigo Vicuna | CFO, Prime Trust

5 hybrid (virtual or in person) instructor-led modules, assessments, networking with leaders from various industries and executive coaching

brainard®
STRATEGY

Brainard Strategy exceeded our expectations assisting us in implementing our first executive leadership development program. The Executives who participated in EXCELerateSM grew significantly as leaders through this robust and vigorous development program. They actively engaged with one another to form new and deeper relationships. Brainard Strategy's EXCELerateSM program has been a catalyst for change in our organization. We have already seen the impact it has had on our executives' direct reports and are excited to watch the impact continue long after the program concludes.

Jeff Filley, President
Behr Paint

Michael Brainard's direct approach and willingness to directly challenge high performing individuals is refreshing. The entire EXCELerate team is excellent – always willing to assist. Most importantly Michael's use of Psychology intermixed with Best in Breed Leadership concepts creates a framework to not only grow during the program but to take those learnings into the months and years ahead – enabling the graduate to continually develop as an Executive Leader.

Richard DeVos
Controller

To learn more about our Stevie Award-winning executive development program, EXCELerate, **navigate to https://www.brainardstrategy.com/excelerate/** or email: **info@brainardstrategy.com**

The program is offered twice per year, in April and September. See you then!

HOW TO BECOME AN EFFECTIVE LEADER

8 DISCIPLINES TO EXCELERATE[SM] YOUR EXECUTIVE LEADERSHIP

Michael Brainard, Ph.D.

Published in the United States by Leaders Press.
www.leaderspress.com

ISBN 978-1-63735-169-7 (pbk)
ISBN 978-1-63735-170-3 (ebook)

SIMON &
SCHUSTER

Print Book Distributed by Simon & Schuster
1230 Avenue of the Americas
New York, NY 10020

Library of Congress Control Number: 2022906089

Thank you, Mykelle, for being an inspiration for your Dad.
I love you and I am fortunate to have a front row seat
as you continue your leadership journey.
You are an amazing young woman, and this book
is dedicated to you and your journey.

Contents

Introduction

IF YOU WERE to ask me why I wrote this book, or why you should read this book, I would answer with the same reason that I opened my consulting firm over a decade ago: to mitigate the impact poor leaders have on corporate America. However, throughout my 25+ years as an executive leader and consultant, I have realized very few leaders actively try to develop as a leader, or even know how to develop themselves as a leader, and further, many are not sure how to mitigate their negative impact on other human beings. While we all know a leader or two who might be the exception to this rule, I have found most leaders are well-intentioned, intelligent people just trying to do their best. So, what gives? Why are there so many ineffective, or even horrible, leaders across organizations?

My hope is that this book can serve as an answer key to the above challenges. I have found once we understand the basis for poor leadership, we can unbundle **both** the process and the content for becoming an effective leader. The 8 disciplines outlined in this book are fundamental disciplines, which leaders across all types of organizations can leverage to ascend in their careers, achieve great enterprise leadership, and harness the power of discomfort to accelerate their growth.

The market is saturated with books and training courses that offer a 10-step approach to becoming a great leader. Simply put, these 'fixes' are a waste of time and money. The truth is, becoming a great leader is not that simple. Authentic leadership development requires **rigor**, a great deal of **discipline** and **practice**, and above all, **deliberate** and **intentional** attitudes, beliefs, and behaviors. Great leadership does not come from simply reading things. Great leadership is the product of intentional experiences gathered over several years. It is far from easy to become a great leader—otherwise, we would have many more effective leaders across our organizations than we do.

While the content of leadership development will be covered in this book, that is only one of two drivers of true development. Many existing leadership books discuss easy and quick leadership frameworks. As a result, complete leadership development is not possible. Unlike existing solutions, this book is intended for the developing leader who is willing to take the tough road ahead. Therefore, this book focuses on not just the *content*, but also the *process* of leadership development. That is to say, this book is anything but a quick and easy 3-step guide to great leadership. Rather, through this book, leaders should move beyond reading and challenge themselves to consider the experiences that will help them achieve true growth. All too often, books focus heavily on the content of what it means to be a great leader, ignoring the rigorous process necessary for effective leadership.

We will explore the study of followership and engagement, the study of the brain, primary research about organizational behavior and leadership development, and my over two and a half decades working with leaders and organizations. The content shared in this book has been researched and practiced extensively. It is not just my point of view—it is fact-based. Unlike other authors, I acknowledge in many cases there is not one simple answer when leading groups of humans. I understand true leadership requires thought, adjustment, and constant practice. This book is the culmination of research, the study of a wide variety of leadership thinkers, and most critically, perspective. I have worked with hundreds of organizations and thousands of leaders across all levels, industries, and types of organizations. The perspectives I have learned, and the insights from those perspectives, are as important—or perhaps even more important—than my research and study of the many facets of leadership development.

By picking up this book, you can become a far better leader than you are today. However, it is unlikely you will ever be a perfect leader. In my 25+ years of experience in working with leaders, I have never met a flawless leader. There are no sugar pills, no quick fixes. If this book works, you will finish reading it and understand what experiences to seek and what content to practice; and you will be humbled with the daunting complexity and discipline required to become a truly effective leader.

Chapter 1

The Discipline of Introspection and "Intro-Action" (YOU)

THROUGHOUT THE YEARS of working with leaders at all levels, I have found two primary root causes of ineffective leadership. The first is insecurity and/or too much ego, and the second is ignorance or the lack of intention to lead. Let's take on the first driver of ineffective leadership. The opposite of insecurity and ego appears to be a leader who is constantly endeavoring for greater self-awareness, the ability to be self-critical, and the nonstop drive toward self-development. It is obvious to think about cases where you have been impacted by leaders who lack self-awareness, are self-protective, and/or who think they have all of the answers.

The second most prevalent driver of highly ineffective leadership is ignorance. These leaders hold onto old beliefs about themselves. These leaders believe their subject matter expertise or technical ability is primary, and dealing with humans is a side project. These individuals have not defined who they are as a leader, nor have they explored how they impact those around them. They haven't made the leap from a highly capable contributor to a leader. In this chapter, we will explore both the content and the process of developing the discipline of self-awareness, self-critique, and self-development, as well as the very difficult work required to develop greater emotional intelligence. We will also explore the process and content for defining oneself as a leader.

EQ

The hard part is the soft stuff. It is so funny for me to hear an ineffective leader talk about the soft stuff as separate from leadership activities and behaviors. For many, the soft stuff is, in fact, the hardest stuff to develop to become an effective leader. Typically, when ineffective leaders speak of the soft stuff, they are speaking of the constructs that make up emotional intelligence. As it turns out, to be emotionally intelligent is the cornerstone of developing the skills required to influence other people as a leader. Emotional intelligence is among the two or three great advances in our thinking around developing leaders in the last 40 years, yet so few people truly understand the concepts. If we consider the concepts of EQ to be the content to strive for, and/or the answer key, then why do so few leaders seek to learn and develop the skills associated with emotional intelligence? In fact, the concepts are simple. The theory that I have formed is that emotional intelligence is not difficult to understand or even to develop. What gets in the way of leaders is arrogance. Arrogance and denial, lead to dismissing the important facts you need to face about yourself to be more emotionally intelligent.

You see, this first step in leadership development is to overcome your insecurities and ego. This requirement demands processes that enable you to develop self-awareness, self-critique, and self-development. The content is not as difficult as the process. Let's define content and process:

- Content is the WHAT
- Process is the HOW

Content is the stuff we talk about and write about in most leadership books. It is the 5-point model so to speak, or the three key values all leaders must have, or a former CEO's definition of leadership.

Process is how one develops. Process activities are reading, introspecting, seeking feedback, endeavoring to challenge oneself. I find that the leadership development literature is filled with content (the *what*), and very few leadership development researchers and practitioners focus on the critical process activities (the *how*). We will explore both in the coming text.

How many of us want to truly transform and challenge how we were raised, or how we were developed by an original dysfunctional boss? How many of us want to do the hard work to tear down existing beliefs and attitudes, that for the most part have served us well—until they haven't? You see, this transformative type of work is what is required and is, in fact, the hard stuff. Then, applying the concepts or content becomes much simpler. The processes like introspection, receiving feedback from others, being willing to be wrong, and seeking to undo beliefs about oneself that may not allow us to be fully influenced are the types of activities that are difficult. I call these 'process activities.' Once in the process of developing, then, one can apply a variety of content to explore. For example, if I'm receiving feedback from others, I should be receiving feedback around 2 to 3 constructs that are easy to understand—like my ability to be self-critical and receive critical feedback. They are the content, but the process is the act of opening oneself up to this feedback.

Process and content begin to converge as we explore a framework for emotional intelligence. The content of Daniel Goleman's model of emotional intelligence includes concepts like self-awareness, self-regulation, self-motivation, empathy, and relationship-building skills.[i] As a developing leader, we know these concepts or this content to be a critical part of the answer key for one's leadership effectiveness. However, the process for becoming more self-aware might include things like being open to feedback, meditating, box breathing, or rigorous introspection. These 'how-to' methods will increase one's self-awareness. Once one endeavors to practice these process activities, the content will be what one learns about oneself. For example, I may have superficially understood that I lack patience or may be a poor listener. But through introspection, I learned the reason for that is because I believe my ideas are better than others' ideas. Through further process activities, like introspection or being open to feedback, I may get deeper into the root cause of that negative behavior. For example, why do I believe that my ideas are better? May I be overly self-protective and fearful of not being viewed as intelligent? That kind of insecurity or lack of vulnerability will certainly impact my ability to influence others. In the above text, we see how process and content, while two different constructs, often work hand-in-hand to enable true leadership development.

What does it mean to be emotionally intelligent? Why is it important? Emotional intelligence (EQ or EI) is a term created by two researchers—Peter Salovey and John Mayer—and popularized by Dan Goleman in his 1995 book of the same name.[ii] EQ is the ability to recognize, understand, and manage our own emotions, as well as recognize, understand, and influence the emotions of others. Goleman was not the first to articulate this concept. However, in his best-selling books—beginning with "Emotional Intelligence" (1995)—the impact on leadership development has been profound.[iii]

For decades, researchers have studied the reasons why a high IQ does not necessarily guarantee success in the classroom or the boardroom. By the 1980s, psychologists and biologists, among others, were focusing on the important roles other skill sets—which are needed to process emotional information—played in promoting worldly success, leadership, personal fulfillment, and happy relationships. In 1990, psychologists Mayer and Salovey theorized that a unitary intelligence underlies those other skill sets. They coined the term, emotional intelligence, which they broke down into four "branches:"

- Identifying emotions on a nonverbal level
- Using emotions to guide cognitive thinking
- Understanding the information emotions convey and the actions emotions generate
- Regulating one's own emotions, for personal benefit and for the common good

Goleman broadened Mayer and Salovey's four-branch system to incorporate five essential elements of EQ. I assert that developing these five elements actually becomes a part of the "answer key" for highly effective leaders.

1. Emotional self-awareness—knowing what one is feeling at any given time and understanding the impact those moods have on others
2. Self-regulation—controlling or redirecting one's emotions; anticipating consequences before acting on impulse
3. Motivation—utilizing emotional factors to achieve goals, enjoy the learning process and persevere in the face of obstacles
4. Empathy—sensing the emotions of others
5. Social skills—managing relationships, inspiring others, and inducing desired responses from them

To test my assertion, let's look at this divergently. We have all worked with highly ineffective leaders. While they may vary in IQ or technical capability, when I have invited audiences of leaders over the past two decades to report the primary attribute of ineffective leaders, I hear themes emerge. Those themes center around a lack of self-awareness, strong values, empathy, relationships, or social skills. While this is not rigorous research, my practical findings overlay nicely with the EQ framework outlined above. The process of developing EQ, and the content of the five essential skills Goleman asserted, becomes a path to effective leadership by positively influencing the people around you. EQ is the closest thing I have found to an answer key to begin the process for one's leadership development. Below, I have outlined a summary of process and content for self-development as a leader from an EQ point of view.

PROCESS (the how of development)	CONTENT (the what to develop)
Feedback (from BOD or 360)	Self-awareness
Introspection	Self-regulation
Coaching	Self-motivation
Counseling	Empathy
Assessments	Relationship skills
Cease old practices	Active listening
Reading	Humility

Intend to Be a Leader

Several years ago, I was introduced to Tom. Tom was a relatively young COO of a mid-sized biotechnology company. Tom had an MBA and a Ph.D. By credentials, he was wonderful. Tom's CEO, who was a bit older and wiser than Tom, asked me to engage as an executive coach for Tom. I asked what the challenges were with Tom and how I could be a resource. My friend, the CEO, smirked at me and said, "Tom's an A-player, except he rubs people the wrong way." I looked at my friend, the CEO, and said, "It doesn't sound like Tom is an A-player, or your grading system is wrong. You can't be an A-player as a leader and rub people the wrong way." The CEO went on to tell me there were significant quality problems where there ought not be in a very simple product line. I endeavored to ask why, and he mentioned there had been some turnover with key talent in that particular production line. When I asked why the key talent left, he said he wasn't really sure, but that HR was compiling the data and he sensed that it had something to do with Tom's leadership style.

So, I set up a meeting with Tom and I asked him a series of questions about his leadership approach and philosophy—pretty innocuous and general questions as we were feeling one another out. About three minutes after I began my questioning around his general approach to leadership and philosophy, he confronted me. He became red in the face, and he looked right at me and said, "Are you implying that I should have some sort of leadership philosophy? I don't have time for that stuff. This is a fast-paced environment and I believe that reacting to the environment is a critical skill, and these people that work for me don't have it." One can easily begin to see the problem with self-awareness, relationship-building skills, general values, as well as his lack of a definition of leadership.

Skipping ahead several weeks, I showed up to debrief Tom's 360 report. I slid the report across the desk and asked Tom to look at the executive summary while I sat quietly. I asked one simple question, "Why do you choose to be an ass?" Tom sat up straight in his chair and said, "Is this how an executive coach talks to the people he works with?" I said, "In some cases, yes, but in most cases, no. According to others' ratings of your leadership effectiveness, you clearly operate to intimidate, to devalue, and to prove you're the smartest person in any room." Tom's peers and direct reports rated him extraordinarily low across these dimensions. So low, in fact, I thought he must be doing this on purpose. So, I pressed a button that I thought would open up an insight—this idea that he is operating this way, as a bully, on purpose. Once Tom got over his defensiveness around my use of the term 'ass,' I asked him to sit quietly for three minutes and answer one simple question, "If you are not intentionally acting in these ways, then why is everyone around you having these perceptions?" Tom was flabbergasted. In this moment, he realized his lack of purpose and intention left him only with his innate personality.

As a young leader, he was able to say he often felt intimidated by some of the senior leaders around him. He sought to overcome this by being rough with people and by being the smartest person in the room. He admitted freely he had no leadership definition and had never even read a leadership book. Tom's lack of intention and deliberateness to lead people left him only with this technical competence. He did not seek to influence, he sought to coerce and force. The people who had to endure his leadership used the words 'bully' and 'ass' in the written section of the 360-degree instrument. But what I found was Tom was not intending to be a bully or an ass. This became an extreme example of where someone who has a lack of intention to lead is then perceived in any way the follower chooses—usually, dictated by the person's personality.

Leadership and leadership development are not about common sense. Tom had tons of IQ and lots of common sense. Tom lacked self-awareness, self-regulation, empathy, relationship building, and a firm definition of who he aspired to be as a leader. Our coaching focused on helping Tom develop processes to increase his self-awareness and empathy. We could not even begin the process work until Tom, for himself, formed the concepts he valued in previous leaders who were highly effective for him. By asking Tom to look at examples of excellent leaders, he was able to define two to three attributes that inspired him. As it turns out, Tom was inspired in the past by being coached and by having a leader care for him and his needs while in graduate school. I simply asked Tom, "Do you think people who consume your leadership would value being coached and cared about?" Tom's insight was rapid, and he began to repair relationships and coach key people. He began to demonstrate caring to all under his pyramid. He put himself through rigorous processes to increase his self-awareness and he learned specific skills to build effective working relationships.

The result of our coaching was that Tom's technical ability and IQ became a great asset for the company, because our end goal was for people in his ecosystem to run toward him with problems and challenges rather than running away from him or hiding those things out of fear. Tom's metric for success was the amount of input he got from others. His belief was that if he got a great deal of input, that was an indicator that he was being vulnerable, approachable, empathetic, and open. Tom's turnaround was dramatic, and Tom's ongoing process to define himself as a leader goes on today. I get emails about once a year where he's excited to tell me about a new leadership attribute he'll focus on going forward, often asking me for resources. Assisting in leadership development in this way and seeing the sort of dramatic turnaround is not regular, but incredibly rewarding as a coach.

Why can't we all be as self-aware or as Emotionally Intelligent as possible? Why are some of us more comfortable in our own skin? The power of three specific cognitive biases...

Hermann von Helmholtz, a 19th century German physicist and physiologist, coined the term "unconscious inference" to describe how an illusion is created within the limitations of our brain.[iv] These early illustrations of visual illusions gave rise to the first pieces of evidence for how our conscious perceptions, which often define our ordinary and subjective experiences, can be misleading. Daniel Simmons' 2011 Ted Talk, *Seeing the World as it Isn't,*[v] highlights how our brain is limited in its ability to perceive data, process data, and subsequently make decisions. The unconscious bias that we possess drives limited perception of the world around us and, therefore, limits our responses to those data.

As leaders, unconscious bias impacts our decision-making in hiring, performance evaluation, talent planning, and promotion, as well as our ability to be innovative and develop high-performing teams. Most importantly, it impacts our ability to see ourselves as we truly are. This self-deception is a root cause for why we are not as self-aware as we wish we could be. By understanding and mitigating the impact of these types of biases, we can become more self-aware and more effective leaders.

Biological Perspective and the Bias Trifecta

Unconscious bias is the first component of what I have found to be The Bias Trifecta, and all Humans possess this primary, innate bias. Rooted in the amygdala, the unconscious mind helps us to process billions of stimuli during any given day. Our brains can quickly decipher which information we should focus on, and we can use this information to survive, make assumptions and inferences, and feel emotions that cause us to be attracted to certain people but not to others.

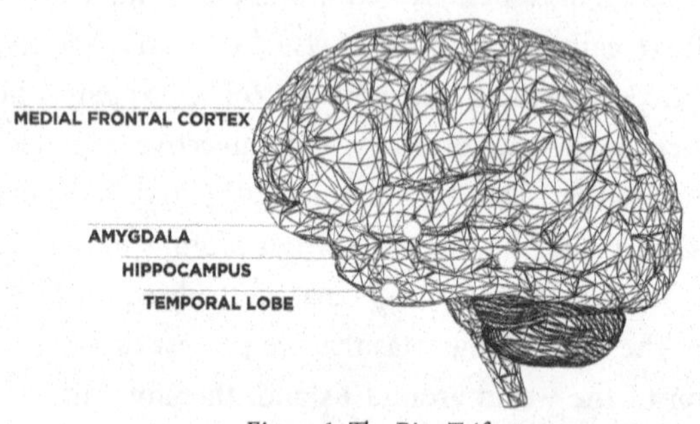

Figure 1. The Bias Trifecta

The amygdala operates based on efficiency and works quickly to process everything going on around us. As a result, we are not completely interpreting all that we see. Our first instincts are based off of these incomplete interpretations and often possess some sort of bias that we are unaware of. This is because the brain does not look for the most comprehensive and holistic interpretation of data, rather, it looks for the fastest and most efficient definition of what a set of stimuli may be. To do this, the impulse must travel through the hippocampus, the part of the brain that is responsible for forming links between memories such as dates and facts and subconsciously steering us toward choosing one option over another. This part of the brain helps us associate stimuli with past experiences, memories, and/or any other information, allowing us to quickly decipher the meaning of the data that we are experiencing. These experiences and memories directly contribute to the way we define or describe a set of stimuli being processed in our brain. While this generally works quite well, the inference is that all of us are victims of our memories, stories, and experiences. Those of us who have long and moderately successful careers tend to believe that our stories, memories, and past successes are the right ones. Therefore, when those impulses are matched to our stories, our certainty can work against us and cause us to make decisions based primarily on our biases.

This leads to the second bias in The Bias Trifecta, **retroactive interference**. Retroactive interference is the influence of after-the-fact experiences on our memory. This concept is highlighted by the work of Elizabeth Loftus, a psychologist at UCI who studies memory mind bugs and the problem with eyewitness testimony in court cases. In one of her more well-known studies (1974), she considers how truly flawed eyewitness testimonies can be. These retroactive inferences also play a role in leadership. I often hear from senior leaders that they are exceptional at hiring talent. When asked why they believe they are excellent, they will reference specific people and highlight their successes. They often fail to acknowledge the number of unsuccessful people who they have also hired in the past. This after-the-fact inference or interpretation of our own behavior happens out of our awareness and seeks to reinforce how right we are. This can make it difficult to recognize and improve upon weaknesses within our organizations and ourselves as leaders. In order to enhance the performance of our organizations at the individual and collective levels, we must first act as disciplined leaders and be able to identify aspects of our experiences that may not be as reliable as we think.

The third component of the bias trifecta is **confirmation bias**. This bias occurs in the left temporal lobe and frontal cortex. The temporal lobe is responsible for information retrieval (tip of tongue) and the integration of sounds and words into meaningful memory. The medial frontal cortex arbitrates decision making, retrieves long term memories, and, most importantly, helps us learn associations between context, location, events, and emotional responses. The medial frontal cortex of our brain is also responsible for rational and logical thought, as well as language.

Confirmation bias is a process during which the brain, in an effort to maintain its aforementioned efficiency, acts in a comparatively apathetic manner. The brain seeks out information in the environment that proves its original thought or memory is correct. This is best exemplified by the business models of MSNBC and Fox News. Neither MSNBC nor Fox News report the news objectively. Their entire business model seeks to present information that demonstrates that their consumer's worldview is, in fact, correct. Leaders exhibiting confirmation bias are often plagued by undisciplined thinking. This undisciplined thinking causes us to reach conclusions more quickly but can also fuel our egos. This is because our brains search for evidence supporting our initial ideas, while overlooking information that supports alternative possibilities. In *Good to Great* (2001), Jim Collins discusses Level V leaders being disciplined of thought.[vi] Leaders who seek only to confirm their worldview is correct limit their learning and limit the sphere of information they have access to.

In summary, unconscious bias, retroactive interference, and confirmation bias work systematically to influence how our brain limits the data we take in, the way we process those data, and the decisions we make based upon those data. It is not an affliction of the majority class; these biases exist in everyone, and we all must work to actively combat the impact of these biases. This is particularly important for those of us with the great responsibility of engaging people in the workplace to drive productive cultures and businesses. As leaders, we must be able to recognize our biases, and also the ways in which they impact our ability to manage our teams. This can be done by increasing our exposure to diverse people and experiences, in addition, not being reliant on one or two dominant stories or memories when processing information. We must develop disciplined thinking techniques to limit our comfort with the "first" answer.

In the Arbinger Institute's book, *Leadership and Self-Deception*,[vii] the authors explore how cognitive biases limit our ability to see ourselves and others in totality. Cognitive biases give us a world view, as well as a self-view, that is distorted. Cognitive biases—and specifically, The Bias Trifecta—impact our ability to be self-aware and self-regulating. These biases act to give us a convenient and satisfying definition of ourselves and those around us. Below, I have outlined a summary of process and content for your development as a leader from the point of view of The Bias Trifecta:

PROCESS (the how of development)	CONTENT (the what to develop)
Emotional intelligence assessments	Educate oneself regarding cognitive bias
Rigorous solo personal challenge	Decision making
Rigorous self-/other-evaluation	Mental toughness
Personality assessments	Empathy
Implicit attitude test	Executive presence
Open yourself up to be challenged	Influencing
Shed "old" self-beliefs	Humility

Our Biases Impact How and Who We Trust

I was once conducting interviews as a part of a team development initiative. As I was interviewing a few of the key leaders, one particular person said, "Those people over in the clinical trials group are untrustworthy." I asked the person to explain how they were untrustworthy. This person, with great detail, explained that this group withheld information, worked around the team leader, and was unresponsive. This person's definition of untrustworthy was based upon the above three observations. I then asked a simple question, "Is everyone on the clinical trials team withholding information, working around the team leader, and being unresponsive?" This person shifted in her seat and said, "Well, not all of them all the time."

So, I asked a follow-up, "Are there any team members in clinical whom you can trust and work closely with?" The person thought for a moment, "I would say maybe five or six." I then asked, "In total, how many people are on the clinical trials team? She said, "Eight."

This is an example of how our biases, specifically, our need for speed and convenience that self-soothe, allow us to quickly put people in a box. *Leadership and Self-Deception*[viii] explores this in great detail, but the implication is far more impactful than this person's observation of the untrustworthy members of the clinical trials team.

You see, because this person's biases were allowing her to very quickly and easily put others into the untrustworthy box, the real impact was she limited her own ability to work with five or six other human beings. Like a smooth spread of paint, she determined that all of them to exhibited the same color (e.g. these three behaviors) and thus, were deemed untrustworthy. The implication is she would behave in a certain, limited way that would, in fact, limit her own effectiveness. I asked her, "Even if you are accurate in your assessment, how does your interaction need to change?" She indignantly said, "I have to protect myself and my other colleagues." I smiled, as this is a very common cause of team dysfunction. Once we define others as something negative, we then give the power to the other person by allowing them to control our interaction. This cycle of defining negatively and, therefore, protecting or acting in a limited way, is a primary cause of team dysfunction. This cycle is a manifestation of our biases negatively impacting our behaviors and interactions. These biases give us the world in a systematically distorted way and, therefore, do not allow us to engage objectively or even in the most effective manner.

Now that we understand the impact of our biases on our EQ and, specifically, our self-awareness, what is another primary reason we are not as effective as we could be? The answer is effective and great leaders need to be deliberate and intentional.

Think for a moment about the most ineffective leaders that have touched your life. Now, ask yourself, were these leaders deliberately and intentionally being evil or ill-willed? In some cases, this may be true, but in the majority of cases a primary driver of ineffective leadership is ignorance. By ignorance, I mean someone ignores the fact that they are to act as a leader. Many highly ineffective leaders don't even define themselves as such. Rather, they define themselves by their occupation. In less extreme cases, we still see people who put leadership as a separate side project while they're doing their 'real job.' In either case, a second primary driver, in addition to ego and insecurity, is a lack of intention or ignorance. So, as we seek to develop ourselves as leaders, let's first be awake and aware that we are given the responsibility to actually ***lead***. In other words, let's be aware that when an organization invites us to manage or lead other humans, it becomes incumbent upon us to accept that challenge in an awake and intentional way.

What does it mean to be intentional? Now that I am intending to lead, what do I do first? I find many experienced and inexperienced leaders share this common mistake. They intend to lead, but they do so using innate skills and/or some early leadership experiences learned from a previous boss (often unwittingly). To be intentional is one thing, but to be deliberate is yet another. What does it mean to be deliberate? To me, it means a person has a solid definition of what it means to be a leader. If I intend to lead, that gets me started. Now, how will I lead in a deliberate fashion? That is answered by having a solid, simple, easily consumable process and developing your leadership definition (content).

To develop a leadership definition, you do not need to go scouring all the leadership books in all the airports across the country. First, let's talk about the process for developing our leadership definition rather than the content. Almost all the literature talks about the content. By content, I mean a framework or a model for a series of attributes. While this is all well and good, very few people talk about the process of leadership development.

First, think of your experiences with great leaders and identify a single attribute which made them the great leader that you remember. For example, many of us have worked with leaders who have demonstrated, above all, compassion, vision, inspiration, coaching, and/or other traits. Then, ask yourself, "Which of these attributes do I possess more naturally, and which must I develop with more rigor?" Second, examine your ecosystem, taking yourself out of the mix, and ask, "What does this group of people and/or teams need from their leader to be most effective?" Similarly, answer this question in the form of single attributes or characteristics. By taking this inside-out and outside-in approach to defining attributes, one can begin to define a set of working attributes that can act as the frame for your leadership definition.

For example, from the inside-out, I have found that respectful candor, having a vision, and being inspirational are attributes that have a particularly positive impact on me and that I would like to strive for. From the outside-in, if I were to depersonalize this, my ecosystem needs toughness, responsiveness, and a coaching approach. So, now I have netted a list of six attributes that will begin to build the frame of my leadership definition. Now, what I might do is go on a fishing trip. By that, I mean I might take those attributes, as undefined as they are, and begin to seek input from others about the effectiveness and desirability of those attributes. Then, I would do rigorous self-examination to determine which of these I have mastered and which I will intend to develop. While the input will be helpful, it will not shape these attributes; I will shape these attributes. In other words, I will settle upon a manageable list of five for a given performance period. I will then set about to operationally define or give myself behavioral examples of what great looks like with regard to each of those attributes. I will then write them in a development plan and identify specific behaviors I will aim to exhibit within those frames.

Now, let's talk about the performance period. An evolved leader will reset this leadership definition approximately once per year. A great time to go through this exercise is around annual planning, strategic planning, or budgeting. This is a natural time when your ecosystem challenges itself and begins to prepare for great performance in the future. An intentional and deliberate leader would use that time to challenge their leadership definition, refine the behavioral attributes, and aim to develop in a very deliberate and specific way around these attributes. Leadership requires hard work, and much like golf, you can never get 18 birdies. Some of these attributes will remain in your leadership definition over many performance periods, and some will disappear and be replaced by newer behavioral attributes based on your ability to master previous ones.

As you can see, I believe the process and the way in which we develop as leaders is far more important than the content. We all know there are about 20 desirable attributes which make a highly effective leader. If you don't believe me, just go buy three or four leadership books in the airport; they all talk about the same 20 attributes. That's not interesting; taking someone else's model is not owning your development. It is most impactful to define the attributes which have been greatly impactful for you and the attributes required from your ecosystem, get outside-in input on what those look like, define specific behaviors, and endeavor to develop for an entire performance period. That is being deliberate about leading and developing as a leader. Mastering those attributes, through introspection, reading, TED talks, and white papers, allows us to narrowly focus on our development in a much more deliberate way. Highly effective leaders are awake and intending to develop in a specific way, enabling them to get better every day. Below, I have outlined a summary of process and content for your development as a leader from the point of view of Your Leadership Definition:

PROCESS (the how of development)	CONTENT (the what to develop)
Define desirable leadership attributes for you	Your Leadership Definition
Define the leadership attributes that your ecosystem needs	Your Leadership Vision
Get outside-in input about your desired leadership attributes (your leadership definition)	The Components of Emotional Intelligence: Self Awareness, Self Regulation, Self Motivation, Empathy and Relationship Building skills
Create your Individual Development Plan (action plan to develop these specific attributes/behaviors)	Ethically-driven Development of Vision and Value
Seek specific articles, TED talks, academic research	Humility as Receptivity to Feedback, Constant Learning, and Growth
Seek situations that demand these attributes	Discernment of Factors Driving Leadership Development
Grade oneself honestly in the early performance period and again at the end of the performance period	Honesty and Accountability Through Metrics and Assessments

Intentional Emotional Intelligence

When I was a young leader, I was fortunate enough to receive 360 feedback. At the time, it didn't feel so fortunate. It was the first time in my career where others rated my leadership effectiveness anonymously. It was a very painful experience. I, like Tom in the previous story, had a belief that common sense, strength, and intellect was all I needed to be an effective leader.

The things I heard about myself were painful. I exhibited behaviors right out of the textbook of being the son of an alcoholic, which I am. I exhibited behaviors of someone who thought intellect was more important than emotional intelligence, and I thought toughness was to be valued overall. You see, I was using my own innate skills as my leadership approach. While that worked well when I was the captain of my high school and college wrestling teams, it did not work well in leading a diverse population of information workers.

I took on this challenge and my own development caused me to seek therapy. I took my own development so seriously that I made a 360 an annual process. I developed my own Board of Directors, a group of two trusted senior leaders who I knew would give it to me straight. I endeavored to find my own definition of effective leadership, and even years later, I still make mistakes against my basic leadership attributes.

My leadership development has been augmented by my study and practice in the actual field of leadership development. I still hold myself accountable for lacking leadership effectiveness in certain situations. I have found leadership development is a never-ending journey. To my knowledge, no one has ever made 18 birdies on 18 holes of golf. I am certain on my own journey, I will never be perfect for all stakeholders, in all situations, at all times. But I have figured out that by being deliberate and intentional, understanding and working the discipline muscles around emotional intelligence, understanding my limitations and being vulnerable and open to input, I can be a person who can influence other people. I can be a leader who engages and energizes the people around me.

Now, I am intentionally leading and being deliberate in my development. This stuff is hard to do every day and requires mental toughness.

As we discussed earlier, some inexperienced or ineffective leaders talk about the soft stuff as if it is somewhat less important than the other stuff. I am often asked, "Why is the soft stuff difficult?" The soft stuff is so difficult because many of us have been over indexed toward mastering our job rather than mastering leadership. It's also difficult because many people lack the mental toughness and discipline to first specifically define the soft stuff they're talking about and second, endeavor to challenge themselves and/or transform themselves to be able to deliver the goods. As an example, it takes mental toughness to think about what a vision even means, let alone to articulate an authentic, easy-to-consume vision for your people. Many people have not framed a cogent vision, yet we know from the engagement literature, connecting people's work to a broader purpose and having a vision as a leader is a key attribute to gaining willing followership. It takes mental toughness to discipline oneself to actually have a vision and do the consistent work to communicate that vision in a meaningful way. It is not work for the faint of heart; it actually takes some mental toughness.

Perhaps more rigorously, mental toughness comes into play when we must transform ourselves at a certain point in our career. Early in our careers, we develop an ego and esteem from having job mastery. At some point in our career, our job mastery is assumed, and leadership effectiveness takes precedence. How often have we watched people miss the opportunity to challenge and transform themselves in deep ways so that they can become more effective leaders? How many of us have gone through the mentally tough work to not have the answer first, but rather, to enable others to have the answer? How many of us have had the mental toughness to not seek to receive the trophy, but to seek to be the one who is offering the reward or trophy? How many of us have gone through the mentally tough work of asking ourselves, "Are we okay with not being the smartest or most accomplished person in our team or department?" How many of us have the mental toughness to focus on leadership attributes that are foreign to us, and as we practice them, we may have to be vulnerable and look and feel silly. Does it really take mental toughness to allow yourself to look and feel silly? I find much of the leadership literature does not speak enough about the mental toughness it takes to transform oneself in a real way to become a better leader.

It takes a great deal of mental toughness to define leadership attributes annually and to focus one's development narrowly on those attributes. In seeking to develop, one learns things about themselves that they don't always want to embrace. A highly effective leader accepts this journey readily. A self-protective, ineffective leader, whom others won't want to follow, often doesn't do the tough work required for this journey. Leadership is not for the faint of heart; it's for the tough. Below, I have outlined a summary of process and content for your development as a leader from the point of view of mental toughness:

PROCESS (the how of development)	CONTENT (the what to develop)
Transform from the job master to the "rookie"	Mental resilience
Practice Mu Shin[1]	Read books about special operators, e.g. SEALs
Meditate	Self-motivation
Challenge oneself to learn something totally new	Self-regulation
Seek critical feedback	Define what transformation means for you
Practice mindfulness	Discipline
Be embarrassed internally by some old beliefs	Humility

The Hard Work of Transformation and Re-Transformation

As this chapter concludes, we have covered two primary causes for ineffective leadership; ego and insecurity being one, and ignorance or lack of intentionality as the second. We have

[1] Mu Shin means 'empty head' or 'no mind' in Japanese and refers to the state of being free from attaching to the mind's contents.

asserted a process to increase self-awareness, self-critique, and self-development is a way to begin intentionality. We have discussed framing one's own definition of leadership as a method to become more deliberate and intentional. We have discussed the importance of being emotionally intelligent and mentally tough. Finally, we have discussed both the content and, more importantly, the process to be a self-improving, self-developing leader. If one endeavors on this path, one must transform. The process of transforming and re-transforming from a manager or individual contributor to an enterprise or executive leader is not for the faint of heart. This chapter seeks to begin the answer to the question Jim Collins implied in his book, *Good to Great*,[ix] which was, "How does one become a Level V leader?"

I am often asked the silly question, "What is the difference between leadership and management?" Management is to guide, control, oversee, regulate, and report. One must manage inside any organization. Leaders find management incredibly easy, as they are able to influence, engage, and motivate individuals and teams. Leaders have vision, strategic thinking, coaching, inspiration, passion, and compassion. Leaders engage, while managers get compliance. To be constantly transforming and re-transforming oneself into a highly effective leader is hard work. I find this work is much more difficult without leadership development planning that happens regularly, good, solid, and trusting feedback loops, and constantly assessing oneself from the outside-in. You'll hear highly ineffective leaders talk about the difference between reality and their perception of themselves. The effective leader knows the only reality that matters is how they are perceived as a leader.

CHAPTER 2

The Discipline of Finding Your Voice and Developing Your Culture and Vision (Projecting YOU)

Creating the Environment for Productivity and Engagement

IN CHAPTER 1 we discussed in great detail the work on one's self that is required to be a truly effective enterprise leader. In Chapter 1 we talked about the key to self-awareness and self-development. We also talked about how to develop emotional intelligence as one seeks to get real, be vulnerable, and be self-motivated. We know these tenants to be critical to engender followership and engagement. But if that were easy and/or enough, being a great leader would be easy and the world would be full of great leaders; we know this not to be true. This book outlines both the process for real leadership development and the content areas to focus on to be a highly effective executive leader in today's organizations. The second discipline to be discussed is the ability for leaders to create the environment for the highest engagement and productivity possible.

A primary root cause of ineffective leadership may also be the leader who is trying to do too much. Yes, this can mean communicating too much, offering too much feedback, running every meeting, and generally overworking. Many of us know these leaders. They are terribly busy. They often have no time for you because they're overwhelmed with the size of their jobs. These ineffective leaders have not thoughtfully created an environment for engagement and productivity. Ultimately, they are using too much hustle and muscle. Whether you're a baseball coach, a corporate executive, or a leader in the military, you will be deemed successful on your ability to create a sustainable environment with the highest possible engagement, as well as exceeding goals around productivity.

A simple formula for highly effective enterprise leaders looks like this:

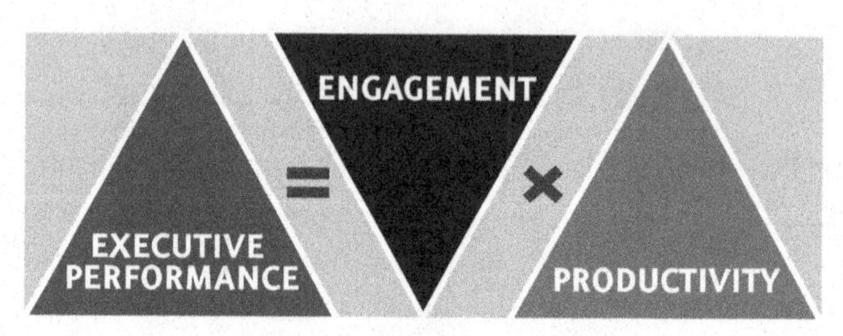

Figure 2. A Simple Formula for Highly Effective Enterprise Leaders

Executive performance is the product of engagement and productivity. You can think about this like a 2 x 2 model. You have all seen environments where you have high motivation and engagement, but low ability to consistently meet or exceed productivity goals. Most of us have also seen environments where we get high productivity, but morale and engagement are quite low. In the simplest form, executive performance can be judged by the ability to drive up engagement and consistently meet or exceed productivity. While there are many skills required to be able to do this, this formula offers a simple model to have a conversation with a developing executive leader that focuses on creating an environment rather than managing person-to-person. You *can* think about this model on the person-to-person level as how do I engage and drive productivity in this one individual, but it's much more effective to think about what I am doing as a senior leader to create the environment where engagement and productivity can occur.

Let's think about creating the environment for high engagement and productivity from the perspective of process and content. The leader who thinks about creating the environment from only a content point of view might be focused on the language and behaviors of leadership. These leaders might tend to overwork as it were. The trap is that I will get the right values in place, get the right behaviors in place and I will have to be on that track of constantly communicating and course correcting. That can be an awful lot of work.

Now let's think about the process point of view around creating an engaged and productive environment. Processes refer to how the work will get done. Have I as a senior leader put in place the right incentive systems, the right communication vehicles, and the right goals, decision authority, and transparent information in a timely fashion? In other words, rather than leading person-to-person, have I built the processes, or what I'll call operating mechanisms, so that people can be productive and engaged without me being present?

When we think about creating the environment for engagement and productivity, we must think about both processes and operating mechanisms that allow people to be productive and engaged as well as the content or the words and meaning that we create around the work. It is one thing to be highly motivated and focused on "the what" is interesting, but if the processes and mechanisms are ineffective we can create a lack of motivation and productivity. If we have great mechanisms and processes but we don't have good communication, direction and focus on the right thing, we also can run into challenges around engagement and productivity.

In summary, let's avoid the mistake of doing too much as a leader. If you have great values in place, if you have created the right environment, and if you have set your ecosystem up so that it can be highly engaging and highly productive, now you can think strategically, coach, and be ready for the next level of leadership.

Operating Mechanisms AND Leader Effectiveness

I was once invited to be the executive coach for a first time CEO in a large manufacturing company. The CEO was eager, positive, and intended to make his mark quickly. He built great relationships and he listened to everyone's challenges and opportunities and made diligent lists. As he did his sensing meetings and built his lists his own to-do list grew exponentially. By the end of his 30th day on the job he was working 60-hour weeks and losing his positive attitude as he became exhausted very quickly. He believed that his behaviors and attitudes and action would win him fans as well as to get him versed deeply in the business. He also believed that at some point he could pull out of this mode and rise to the level where he should be playing, but he felt stuck at the 90th day. He was still in the same place of overwork and exhaustion. It seemed to him that every time he corrected a problem or got involved, there were other challenges and other places to be involved. It seemed never ending.

Upon meeting him around the 90-day mark I asked to see his monthly calendar and I asked him to print out a calendar for the next 12 months. He looked confused as he didn't have much on the calendar except for a board meeting two months from now, but other than that, the calendar had a lot of blank open space on it. Looking out a week or two showed that he was overbooked in a given day and in specific weeks. I asked the CEO where his operating mechanisms were and where his various teams participating in those mechanisms were showing up. You can imagine the way he looked at me. He didn't know what operating systems were. He hadn't identified teams to take up much of the important and strategic work to come. He got lost in those early sensing interviews and all of the various tasks that he intended to do in the short term and pull out of it in a long term. The problem was as he kept opening doors, his to-do list kept growing and the idea that he could sit down and plan out for a quarter or a year disappeared.

We discussed the typical mechanisms, like operational efficiencies, strategic planning, tactical reviews of key projects, and client and external sensing mechanisms. We endeavored to design a series of interactions with key talent and key teams around each of those mechanisms. We challenged the leaders of those teams to present to the CEO, bringing him up to speed and offering a series of action items that they would take on for the next quarterly Sprint. In this particular case we decided that the operational reviews should occur monthly. We also decided that there were three key projects that would make or break his success and how he would get a readout and review of those in advance of the operational meetings. We had three placeholders for strategy to occur and even for the board to be involved in those strategic reviews.

Once we set this infrastructure in place or these operating mechanisms, he was able to have a place to house these critical functions. The last thing we needed to do was to delegate to key leaders some of the tasks that the CEO was involved in and to allay his concern about giving up those tasks, we built a series of one-on-ones not only with these direct reports but with key talent responsible for those tasks. These 15-minute and 30-minute stand up meetings allowed him to remove himself from doing and place himself as a coach. This transformation, if it doesn't occur rapidly, can lead to the demise of a well-intended CEO.

Create and Align

So now we're thinking more about creating an environment for engagement and productivity rather than pushing the boulder uphill every day when we come to the office. The environment, if thought about strategically, can act as a tailwind for leadership effectiveness. For me, this is critical and I've often watched leaders struggle with this—in fact, I too have struggled with it. Specifically, the struggle centers around how we create an environment with high engagement and productivity. On the one hand, building the right operating mechanisms and processes is not that difficult, even though it does take some thought. But an insight I've come to is that it can be summarized as CVS. Not the pharmacy chain, but rather the infra-structure is: Culture, Vision, and Strategy.

CVS

First, to create the environment for the highest possible engagement and productivity, one does not have to think about everything. I have found the best approach is to invite leaders to think about, have a voice around, and put incentives around Culture, Vision, and Strategy.

Let's define our terms. Edgar Schein, who spent his life studying culture and performance, gave us the definition of culture that is most easy to understand. Culture is "the way things get done around here."[x] We all know that values act as behavioral anchors for culture. If one has articulated and specifically defined core values, then we have created the front end of culture, or the desired state of our culture. The outcome of how work actually gets done requires modeling and incentives. As a highly effective leader, have we specifically been thoughtful about the kind of culture we want to create and articulated that through core values and stories? Have we put formal and informal incentives in place to drive toward the kind of culture we want? Many ineffective leaders sometimes think this work is too esoteric and conceptual. These leaders are simply immature and will be stuck in the kneecap stage of management for the rest of their careers. To have a voice, to model, and to incentivize culture is to create a tailwind for engagement and performance because how we do our work often is critical to predicting what we will produce and how effective we will be.

Second, one must take a similar approach with Vision. Many ineffective leaders think vision is something that is the sole realm of the CEO. In other words, many ineffective leaders think it's not their job to have a vision. We know that leaders who have a vision get high engagement and can attach people's efforts to a greater cause. Having a vision does not mean you want to talk about world peace, but rather having a vision means that you can articulate what winning or success looks like for an individual, for your environment and for your ecosystem. In short, have you articulated in some logical period of time what success looks like for the individuals and teams in your ecosystem? And can you connect people's efforts to that success?

Burt Nanus has talked about visionary leaders in his work and he talks about the roles senior leaders must play to be visionary.[xi] In more simplistic terms, having a vision means that I have articulated what success or winning looks like for my ecosystem and connected that to their efforts.

So, if I have had a voice and I have modeled the behaviors on the culture of how things get done around here and I have articulated what winning or success looks like for my ecosystem, the next question becomes how. Think about strategy in answering how we will win or succeed. Again, many ineffective leaders abdicate this responsibility and think strategy is the job of the C-suite. It is, and it is also the job of you as a leader to articulate in its absence or to translate when it exists for my ecosystem. Imagine the highly effective leader who has described the similarities and differences of his or her culture relative to the macro culture. Imagine the leader who has described what success looks like specifically for their ecosystem and how it is aligned or not aligned with the larger organization or system. Now think about the leader who can look up at the corporate organizational strategy and translate from it the specific strategy for that leader's group to be highly effective and engaged. With that image in mind, you can see how effective leaders can be once they have successfully communicated and translated their vision.

LBI

When I think about any leader at any level seeking to have greater impact, two simple models can best summarize the above. When creating an environment for high engagement and productivity, one must use the only and oldest and most tried-and-true influencing model there is: LBI—Language, Behavior, and Incentives.

There are only three ways to influence human beings and they are by using your own language, by modeling your own behaviors, and by offering incentives. Every leader must know that the LBI Model can be applied to how we create winning teams.

When defining modeling and incentivizing culture, think about specifically articulating your vision and behaving consistently with that vision while incentivizing success and engagement. Then, a leader can consistently talk about strategy, hold oneself accountable for and behave consistently with that strategy, and incentivize the right outcomes. This leader can then get far down the road in creating the environment for the highest possible engagement and productivity. Clearly articulating, behaving, and incentivizing on these three dimensions (CVS) allows one to begin to create and cultivate an environment where daily management becomes unnecessary. Your work at this point becomes like that of a chiropractor. Because environments are always changing and humans are always changing, one must now make sure we have alignment not only around CVS but also alignment and consistency of approach around LBI. This act of constantly tailoring, correcting, and adjusting to external as well as internal forces then becomes the work of the enterprise leader. Now imagine the leader who has not had a voice on culture, vision, and strategy. How much more work does that leader have to do to align large groups of humans with good intentions?

I would like to assert a very simple hourglass model here. Any highly effective leader is applying the hourglass model to culture, vision, and strategy. They're looking upward and collecting key information about culture, vision, and strategy from the larger system within which they work. They're pulling that information into themselves and translating it, putting their own fingerprints on it, and doing the hard work of repackaging it in such a way that their particular ecosystem going downward can engage and be productive. The hourglass model is a highly effective model to keep you as a leader both aligned with the larger system and engaged with your ecosystem.

Figure 3. Insinuating the Hourglass Alignment Model

We can all think of a person with whom we've worked in the past who wants to fight City Hall. This person comes in with their own strategy, disagrees with the strategy of the larger system, and even gets negative toward it. Ultimately the culture will win, and that person will be eliminated from the system. The hourglass model seeks to avoid that—it's a mechanism to constantly assess how far aligned or out of alignment I am with the macro system. What am I doing to align and engage my ecosystems with the macro system? Asking where I am aligned or not aligned is a constant exercise that an effective leader endeavors upon.

So, after getting ourselves transformed to more effectively lead, the second step becomes asking the following question: Have I created the environment for the highest possible engagement and productivity? I have found that highly effective leaders have a voice, have a model, and have put the right incentives in place around culture, vision, and strategy.

By using the LBI Model when applying culture, vision, and strategy, aligning with the macro system, and engaging their resources and people, the effective leader has a unique environment where engagement and productivity are more likely to occur. We will always have individual differences and we will always have shifting internal and external environments, so this aligning mechanism becomes critical. While there is much more to do to be a highly effective enterprise leader, not getting the environment in place is a classic mistake of the ineffective leader or the leader who is stuck in their career.

PROCESS	CONTENT
EP=E*P	Language
Hourglass model	Behavior
Creating environment	Informal incentives
Formal incentive systems	Values
Strategy of the system	Your translated strategy

The second discipline discussed in this chapter was the discipline to NOT DO EVERYTHING, rather to create the environment for the highest engagement and productivity possible. All effective leaders must build the environment where the very highest engagement and productivity can occur. A way to think about that is to intentionally and actively build Culture, Vision, and Strategy and to then reinforce those things through Language, Behavior, and Incentives.

CHAPTER 3

The Discipline of Influencing With or Without Charisma

IN CHAPTER 1, we discussed the importance of developing processes to increase one's self-awareness, its ability to be self-critical and to enhance self-development. We also discussed the idea of highly effective leaders being intentional and deliberate. Specifically, we described the process for defining desired attributes and focusing one's development for one solid year, or another specific performance period. In Chapter 2 we discussed establishing an environment that will enable engagement and productivity. Specifically, we discussed our model for translating and communicating culture, vision, and strategy. In Chapter 3, we will discuss influencing or leading without authority or power.

I often get the question: Do I have to be charismatic to be a senior leader? Do extroverts make better leaders and introverts?

I find these questions entertaining, as I have researched and more importantly practiced leadership development for the last 20 years. I have found charisma to be only moderately helpful in some situations. But it's not the defining attribute for a highly effective leader. Many ineffective leaders make the assumption that charisma, and or being outgoing, is a dominant or primary leadership skill. I have had the great pleasure of working with highly effective leaders who may be introverted, or even struggle to speak publicly at times. As mentioned in Chapter 2, there are only three ways to influence a human beings: language, behaviors, and incentives.

With or without charisma, all humans have to communicate effectively to engender followership. While this book will not dive deep into communication skills, the effective articulation of concepts and ideas, being able to put ideas together so that others can find meaning and/or be easily influenced by them is a critical skill. Let's take the extreme example of Mr. Charismatic. Mr. Charismatic may use too many words, lack authenticity, and overwhelm us with complexity. A more introverted leader, or one who lacks natural charisma, may be efficient with words—meaning what he says and saying what he means—and be able to adjust the message for a variety of audiences. There is nothing inherently wrong with the use of language and communication. It is a learned behavior, honed with discipline and practice.

The second way to influence other human beings is to model behavior. Adult learning theory reminds us that modeling behavior is a critical way to teach and to have an influence in organizations. Being aware of our behaviors and showing up consistently aligned with our words and values allows others to easily attach to us without question, confusion, or lack of trust. By modeling and demonstrating behaviors, other humans can quickly learn and adjust their behaviors if so desired. We all have obvious examples of hypocritical leaders. Leaders who might say for example, "We're all in and we must work around the clock to deliver this particular project." Then, we see that leader leaving at 4:30 with golf clubs in tow.

In 2011, McKinsey and Aegon Zender did a study of highly effective leaders.[xii] In this study, they show that leaders gain reputation and increase their effectiveness, not talking great all the time, but by showing up in spiky moments. A spiky moment is a moment of great impact, or a moment that has a long tail. The leader models behavior in times of transition, change, or crisis. They enjoy great followership without demanding.

A third way to influence human beings is through incentives. We think of incentives as rewards or consequences for types of behavior, attitudes and language. An environment that informally incents these things, as well as formally incents certain behaviors, is an environment where culture can be deliberately fostered. If I inadvertently incent the "hero" behavior, I am communicating to the broader organization that lack of preparation and hero behavior is valued. This common mistake of leaders—that is, in incentivizing hero behavior—is often out of a lack of awareness. It's a great example of where we can see incentives being very powerful forms of leadership for the good and not so good.

Don't Withhold the Answer Key

Combining the LBI framework with the blunt force that comes from repetition allows for leaders to enable followership. Consistency and reputation around our core values, consistency of behavior around the desired behaviors and the core values, and the intrinsic and extrinsic rewarding of desired behaviors and performance to values shows employees and management how to win and succeed in any culture. Before a leader gets too fancy with language and technique they have to be followable and one of the ways that we engender followership is the consistency in our language, our behaviors, and what we incent. Consistency gives followers the ability to understand and even replicate those desired behaviors. Of course, a leader will react in many directions daily and weekly, but to come back to that center point: For my own journey on an annual basis, I'll set about to put the right language around the desired behaviors required to accomplish our goals.

By NOT defining specific desired culture attributes, a vision for success for "us," and a clear strategy so that all can achieve their goals, we are hamstringing the performance and engagement of our people.

One year for a whole year we just talked about respectful candor and it helped me to be candid, supportive, and respectful. I began to hear other people use term respectful candor and wrestle with what it meant and give each other feedback around respectful candor. As the leader, we can't be shy about asserting these words or this language. It will catch on with people who want to succeed as leaders through their modeling of behaviors, their use of language, and their incentives. It will allow people to find the winning formula. By withholding consistent language and incentives, you're not providing followers with the means to get an A on the paper. Leadership in organizations is not like high school. In high school, teachers ask you to read the chapters, they tell you what's on the test, and lo and behold, the two questions you got wrong were from the chapter you didn't read. We can't operate corporations, companies, and organizations like that. We want to show people how to get an A on the paper. The CVS and LBI frameworks shows people how to get an A on many more transactions than they otherwise might if leaders are not clear about CVS and LBI.

By aligning our language, behaviors, and incentives, we can then influence individuals, groups, and teams. Messaging is one way to influence individuals, but showing up as a leader when it's time to show up and rewarding desired behaviors to get engagement and productivity are key influencing tactics for all leaders. I find the process for developing language around desired behaviors more important than the content or what those actual behaviors are. I find the process for thinking about formal and informal rewards far more important than what those rewards actually are. A leader who is awake and intentional will think about language, her own behaviors and informal forms of reward and punishment actively. By putting into practice the LBI Model, we can increase our ability to influence without power.

The Golden Circle

A second key construct around influencing without power was given to us by Simon Sinek. Sinek shared his insight during a 2011 talk.[xiii] His insight is that if we as leaders seek to align followership and get engagement, we can communicate from the inside of our brains to the outside. We can have greater influence and attract people who believe what we believe. By speaking to the emotional part of the brain, you can align their "why" to our "why." Sinek talks about the why, then the how, then the what as a communication model. I have put this into practice for many years as a consultant and can attest to the direct difference in followership by following the Golden Circle. Decision-making is held in the emotional part of the brain, specifically the amygdala of our lizard brain. People make decisions like following you, or being influenced by you, or buying what you're selling in this part of the brain. Communicating at that level around why something is important to all of us—for me and for you—is far more important than indicating a list of features and benefits. I find reminding senior leaders to lead with the why and conclude with the what helps those leaders engender followership and gain deeper engagement.

We know from the study of employee engagement something about followership. Engagement seems to be driven by: One, relationship with the boss. Two, relationships with peers. Three, meaningfulness of work. Fair and aligned incentives are also required. To lead with influence and not power then requires us as leaders to invest in relationship skills and relational capital with our constituents. One does not have to be a relationship expert. Rather, relationship skills are learned sets of skills.

As a leader, to get engagement and my peers' trust, I need to engage with them. In this way, I can increase engagement and influence. Additionally, I need to have everyone in my organization working on meaningful outcomes. In other words, does my work really matter?

If I want to influence without power, I must seek to get engagement from all in my ecosystem. I do this by setting up processes like pay systems, performance rating systems, and promotion systems that are fair and equitable. I also do this with my language, behaviors, and the content of my interactions. In this way, we can see that both process and content are required to set up an environment for influencing, without authority taking hold.

Relational Capital

In the previous sections we discussed influencing without power being contingent upon the LBI framework and the ability to get engagement, using communication techniques like the Golden Circle and understanding the drivers of engagement. As we do those things, we increase our relational capital. I find that great leaders are aware of investing in relationships. I often say that being a great leader is to be friendly and warm, not to have lots of friends. To invest in relationships is not to be touchy-feely. Rather, any leader knows that if you want engagement from others you must invest in the relationship.

I find great leaders to be net exporters in all cases. If we look back at the construct of emotional intelligence, we find one concept called self-motivation. Great leaders don't look to the outside world to be motivated; they are an exporter of motivation. Regardless of circumstance, regardless of the personality type of the other, I can always find something important in another person and or a reason to invest in a relationship. The leader who is turned off by someone's personality or behaves differently because of external situations is a weak leader. The highly effective leader is unfazed by the other person or ecosystem and rises above, and as the mental toughness has a positive and productive affect, even on the most unseemly types of people. Building relational capital requires mental toughness. It's easy to dismiss others, particularly if they don't share your thoughts. It's difficult to find common ground, to identify with, and to find it important to engage with all people in an ecosystem. Relational capital should be derived from a great deal of investment and may never even yield a return for you. But the leader who is not self-protective and exports motivation often is a leader many will follow.

Integrative Negotiation

As leaders, we are all negotiating for resources, talent and to get things done in the most effective way. I find that negotiating in an integrative manner rather than distributive often leads to relational capital and shows leadership using influence rather than power. Distributive negotiation is that type of negotiating that looks like buying a car at a car dealership, where one size wins and one side loses. Integrative negotiation is finding the zone of all possibilities, negotiating the best alternative outcome for both parties, and finding the "win/win." Thinking about debating for resources and talent—and setting up debates in general where one side wins and one side loses—is a fool's game when trying to have an influence. Thinking about integrative approaches to resource conversations offers the potential for all sides to get something if not today, then tomorrow. It's a way to gain influence without power.

Think about this. The insecure or effective leader is self-protective and wants to win or even look good in front of peers. This is a natural human tendency. It's not a tendency for a highly effective leader. The highly effective leader is willing to be vulnerable, doesn't need to be self-protective, and often exports information resources and talent readily. This type of net exportation and integrative negotiation requires great mental toughness and security. But the net giver is the one who has relational equity, leads without power, and is highly influential. The tendency to be protective and defend one's turf is the realm of the unit leader. It takes great mental toughness to be the giver, but this person often has a great deal more influence than the insecure.

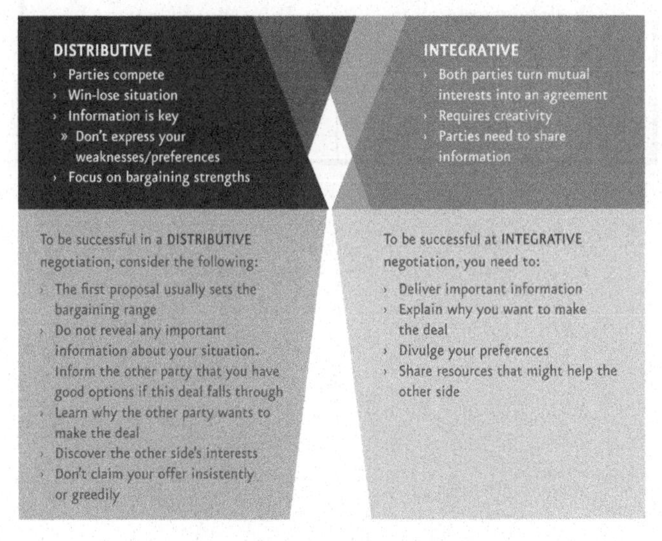

Figure 4. Distributive vs Integrative Negotiation[xiv]

In summary, LBI, the Golden Circle, relational equity, and integrative negotiating are specific techniques to allow one to influence without power; to allow one to have a net of people around who have felt invested in and engaged. A highly effective leader has people around them who want to be supportive and build them up when not present. These influencing techniques can be practiced and learned. With discipline, one can gain influencing skills regardless of extraversion or charisma. The discipline of leading with influence is the realm of the highly effective leader and not the work of a self-protective, insecure person.

PROCESS	**CONTENT**
Discover your source for authenticity	Assess for Extroversion or Introversion
Uncover your "why"	What is your natural negotiating style
Challenge yourself to "revalue" relationships	Why should anyone be inspired by me today?
Ignore your position power	What can you give to others daily?

CHAPTER 4

Coaching: The Discipline of ENABLING Productivity and Performance

Leading in an Organization

IN CHAPTER 1 we discussed the deliberate and intentional ways to increase self-awareness, self-critique, and self-development in both the process and content. In Chapter 2 we discussed highly effective leaders creating an environment of engagement and productivity. For Chapter 3 we discussed how highly effective leaders influence without power. In Chapter 4 we will specifically discuss coaching as a superpower. Coaching is a discipline and practice to challenge and change performance in other people. Coaching is a form of influencing that is targeted and meant to enhance the lives and careers of those around the leader. Having competence and confidence to challenge yourself to be a coach as well as a leader and then holding those skills over a lifetime is required for highly effective enterprise leaders.

Competence and Confidence and How It Impacts Your "Out-of-Balance" Player/Coach Ratio

I find that many leaders who are too busy are in fact being ineffective leaders. Busy-ness is a choice. And what to be busy on requires discipline. I often find leaders who cannot make the transition from doing to leading or coaching often cease to develop. The driver that causes us to be out of balance as we transition to greater leadership roles is often insecurity. Think about it this way: The insecure leader often has years of job mastery behind them. So when something of importance must really get done, the insecure leader goes backwards into their skill set and goes downward to do the job of others. In so doing, that leader gains esteem and a sense of achievement for accomplishing some task or set of tasks. This is the height of insecurity. Because I'm insecure in my ability to lead a coach or set up the right processes for others to perform at a high level, I hop backwards to that place of expertise and do rather than coach.

The competence required to coach others is not there yet, but the competence to accomplish tasks is. So instead of challenging oneself to move forward into a lead and coach role in a less-than-perfect way, the insecure leader goes backwards to that place in their career where they do many things very well. The result of this can be disempowering for the people whom they lead and who should be given the challenge and the coaching to accomplish those same tasks. The confidence to lead and the confidence to let go is a critical crucible for the discipline leader to manage.

An exercise to help you determine your own ratio for doing versus leading goes as follows: On a sheet of paper, draw a circle on the left and a circle on the right. On the left divide the circle based on the actual time spent doing versus leading. Then, with the circle on the right, divide the pie with your desired ratio of doing versus coaching. By desired, I mean your optimal amount in your leadership role. By examining the difference between the current state and the desired state of playing versus coaching, we can begin to be mindful about how much more time we need to dedicate to leading, coaching, and managing versus doing or playing. I find this exercise often surprises people with its simplicity and the insight gained. Again, it takes competence knowing how to lead a coach and it takes time and ability to lead a coach as they transition to an enterprise leader. Throughout this section, we will talk specifically about coaching skills and how to challenge and change behavior in others.

Productivity versus Performance

The ineffective leader often seeks to coach productivity rather than performance. Productivity is defined as the ratio of outputs to inputs. It's the scoreboard. The reactive leader responds to the backwards set of scores. The proactive or effective leader coaches for performance, or how people do what they do. One of the first things we do when thinking about coaching is we ask ourselves, "What do we coach?" and "Why do we coach?" The highly effective leader knows that performance is often by the how. We coach behaviors and attributes rather than numbers and outcomes.

Second, why do we coach? We coach because we care. We care, therefore we are compelled to facilitate the challenge or change of behaviors and/or approach, thus allowing a person to grow and develop while building organizational capacity. We will define coaching in a moment, but these antecedents are required to set up a coaching environment. The first antecedent is *what do we coach to?* The answer is we coach behaviors and attributes, not outcomes. The second antecedent is *why do we coach?* If we cannot care about the situation or the person, it is very difficult to coach. We coach because we care about the person and or the situation and want to challenge or affect some change in the person or situation.

So if that is what we coach to and why we coach, then what is coaching? ***Coaching is a facilitated process for self-development*** in others. Let's break that sentence down. Coaching is to facilitate or promote in others the ability to gain insight without giving advice. Coaching is a process, not an event. In other words, effective coaching occurs over time in many different situations, all centered around key behavioral action or aspects that will help a person perform sustainably over a long time. Coaching enables self-insight or self-development. We know about human motivation. Humans are much more motivated to implement their own ideas or their own insights rather than an outside set of insights or an outside suggestions. This enables them to gain insight as they facilitate the process, and challenge themselves as the job coach. Management is about telling and advising. Coaching is about facilitating self-development and insight through process interactions. While coaching may be slow and at times even inefficient, great leaders invest in coaching because it brings about sustainable behavior change and an increase in the person's capability.

Segmenting Performers and Defining Your "ROI" for Coaching

Many leaders have great experiences with coaching and often not so great experiences with coaching. One of the reasons is that coaching is a set of skills that is difficult to be great at. So the first insight for a great coach is that they may not be a great coach. Therefore, when we don't see a change in behavior in the person where the coaching is quick, the tendency can be to blame and/or assume that they don't have the innate talent. Until you are the world's greatest coach, you are unable to say that. Because I can take that same person and give them a great coach and you will see a change in their behavior. The first construct in becoming a great coach is to realize that you are singularly accountable for the career performance of people in your ecosystem. When you take that accountability and you hone your coaching skills, you assume that you have some requisite level of coaching skill, and you can hold others accountable for not making challenges or change occur.

So let's assume for a moment that you are a great coach. You can demonstrate that by segmenting the performance of individuals and teams in your ecosystem so you can gain greater insight into the coaching process and coaching outcomes. As an example, when coaching an A performer, the coach often finds a self-critical person eager to get better. When coaching a C performer, one finds defensiveness and blaming in many cases. Therefore, the coach must be able to handle defensiveness, and bring the coaching conversation back to the person being coached. Sometimes we blame the person's work coaching on a lack of change rather than simply understanding the differences in types of people and type of behavior they were trying to coach.

A leader who establishes a coaching culture has segmented objectively and accurately the performance of their key talent and key teams. We look at individuals and teams as units of productivity, not being perfect. If we can objectively and accurately assess them using something like a letter system, we can significantly enhance our targeted coaching. Any vibrant ecosystem is gaining and losing "cells" every day. A leader who establishes a coaching culture has segmented performance accurately and creates mobility in the ecosystem. Many A players are challenged to grow and develop into different roles and different jobs. They are challenged to become A players and are given specific targeted coaching to get there. For that to occur, the coach had to honestly assess the ability of a player so they can be challenged and changed in specific terms and have a chance to become an A. As you're reading this, I hope you're asking: "Have I segmented performance of my ecosystem at the individual level and the team level so that I can honestly coach to specific traits, enabling a seed to move to a B, perhaps eventually to an A, and a D player to perhaps move out the organization?"

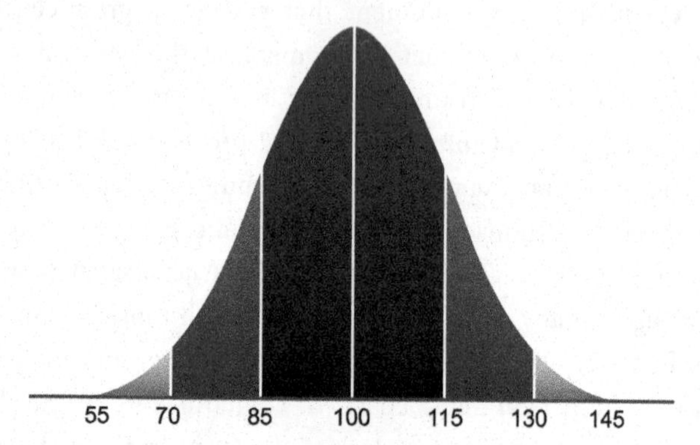

Figure 5. A Sample Normal Distribution Curve of Team and Individual Performance Levels

The strong coach needs to constantly assess the performance of the teams and individuals accurately and objectively. Secondly, the highly effective coach then has to find specific attributes for teams and individuals to improve upon to move or become mobile. Then the third step is to coach for mobility. So I have a young C player who has 2 to 3 specific attributes to improve upon so they might become a B player. I sat down with them and specifically outlined what she looks like relative to a C. Have I invited a person to gain some insight as to why it might be important to focus on these attributes and how they might go about demonstrating improvement upon those attributes? As a coach, I hold that one for last and hopefully I never have to mention "the what" because if the individual can determine what to do differently to practice new behaviors, then they own the practice.

Getting them to own the practice and being motivated to make the change, that is the job of the coach. Most people do not need to be told the answer. The answer is often known and less important than the motivation to change. Think about this easy to remember formula:

P = M * A—Performance equals Motivation times Ability

Performance equals Motivation times Ability. In other words, one's performance is the product of one's ability and one's motivation. As an example, if you were to play golf, you might develop a slice. A slice is when the ball comes off your club and radically moves away from a straight line. While walking through the airport, you see a picture of Phil Mickelson with the caption on the cover of the Golf that says, "Four easy steps to cure your slice." You read the four steps and in fact they are easy (the content). So when you step onto the driving range and you implement the steps, the ball goes straight. However, when you move to the golf course and continue hitting the ball, the slice returns. Implementing the answer is just like that. You might get immediate satisfaction or an uptick in short-term ability. But you must have the motivation to stand on the driving range for hours at a time and grow new muscle memory around those four steps (the process). In other words, without the motivation to ingrain the change, the change is not sustainable. Performance is ability multiplied by one's motivation. When I'm coaching, I often assess both motivation and ability and invite people to make upticks or to challenge their current ability as well as their current motivation to change.

An ineffective leader and coach is over-indexed around ability. They will outsource the coaching to a training course or an article. One does not do great by reading articles or books. One gets great by being motivated to do the hard work to develop new skills, new habits and self-motivation. When I coach, I challenge the person's motivation to want to do the work to change over offering the answer. A great coach is a great motivator. Answers are easy. Motivation is difficult.

The Coaching Model

So now we've discussed what we coach, which are behaviors. We coach when we care about a person or situation and we want to challenge or change behavior. And finally, we coach performance, which is a blend of ability—and more critically, one's motivation. A highly effective leader uses framework shortcuts. Coaching lends itself perfectly to this. A great leader seeking to be a great coach will help someone to look inward at themselves, outward at their environment, and help that person develop a plan to move forward. This inward, outward, and forward model is the world's most simple coaching framework. A coach is constantly inviting someone to look inside at their traits and attributes that are driving the behaviors that need to be challenged or changed.

A great coach is constantly cleaning the lens of the people they're coaching so they see their outside world more accurately. And a great coach has a contract with people they coach to focus on the highest value targets or the 1 to 3 key behaviors to be challenged or changed over a period of time. A great coach works on one's motivation to want to improve and challenge and change.

Figure 6. Looking Inward, Outward, and Forward Coaching Model

The process for questioning and coaching is far more important than the content or the topic on which we coach. As an example, a great coach has many methods to help one look at oneself differently to gain insight. The ability to gain insight is critical, regardless of the topic one is gaining insight on. This process approach to coaching helps one to look inside of themselves and outside to their environment, and helps one develop their own plan for moving forward. This is the important work of a coach. As a coach, you could identify the specific attribute for the person to work on. But in fact, a great coach would avoid naming the behavior or attribute to be improved. Rather, the great coach would help the person self-discover the behavior or attribute to be improved. Coaching is the classic example where the process and the model is far more important than the content or what we're coaching to.

Bob's Blame Game

When I was introduced to Bob as an executive coach, I was immediately impressed by Bob's superior intellect, and his need to be seen as someone with superior intellect. Bob led from a position of authority that came from technical expertise and many of the engineers who worked with him greatly appreciated his technical expertise. Bob was a highly effective manager but people would leave his organization regularly as he wasn't the warmest and fuzziest person. When Bob was asked to take on an executive coach because of his lack of warmth, and because of turnover issues throughout the engineering organization, he was perplexed. He had made the assumption that people were leaving his organization because they weren't intellectually up to the task of working there. He almost had a sense of pride around the turnover.

Following the inward, outward, and forward model, I started by asking Bob a series of questions about how he actually felt about people leaving his organization, who would go to other organizations and be successful. I asked Bob if being viewed as successful by his group was important to him. Of course he said yes. I asked Bob what he thought his reputation was outside of the engineering organization. I mostly asked Bob the difference between how he felt and what he tended to do, versus what was happening around him. Bob was over-indexed on blaming the ones who left for not being up to the task, or for blaming the organization for not paying his people properly, or for blaming anyone in the environment for anything. Bob's core challenge was that he was not self-critical. He was an external thinker. When Bob came to count the examples of how many times others were wrong or had wronged him, he paused and turned visibly red. He said, "Oh my gosh, I think I see what you're asking me. You're asking me to take some responsibility for these five or six challenges that we've just identified." I quickly said, "No, I'm actually not asking that. I'm simply asking you to look inside yourself and ask yourself, why are you not comfortable taking responsibility or even blaming yourself for some of these five or six challenges that are happening around you. What about you is blocking your heart from accepting that responsibility, and causes you to blame the external world for some of your leadership challenges?"

Bob pondered why he was unable to blame himself; why he wasn't allowing his heart to accept the responsibility. Getting to that understanding would stick with Bob forever. He was now beginning to develop a comfort with being wrong, or even potentially being wrong. With that, he could then look into the world with a slightly more accurate view and begin to view the challenges the organization was driving for the engineering team, and some of the challenges he was driving for the engineering team, in a much more balanced way. He was now able to balance looking inward and looking outward to find a more accurate set of challenges and causes so that he could move forward in a more objective and rational way. While Bob took a lot of pride in being objective and rational, in fact it was his defense mechanism to externalize that allowed him to view the world in a deluded and even unobjective way. Helping Bob look inward not at one challenge but at the impulse to protect himself and not take his part in challenges was the coaching he needed. We used five or six challenges as themes to ask the broader question about what was going on inside for Bob.

Getting the Front-End Correct

Get in balance with the "what" and "how"—setting expectations and why expectations matter far more than setting goals.

As we can see from the story of Bob, the process of questioning and helping somebody look inside, outside, and develop their own plan to move forward is a critical skill for any coach. A second skill is getting the front right. By that I mean enabling the person to focus on the critical 1-2 and no more than 3 behavioral attributes or coaching goals. Just like one's own leadership development, letting these expectations and goals remain in place for about a year allows the person being coached to go deep into a focused and targeted set of high-value growth targets. An ineffective coach is constantly changing and moving the targets for success. Allow the person you're coaching to be thoughtful and to go deep into one or two areas in a given performance period. And no more. This discipline requires a great coach.

Once we have implemented the world's most simple coaching model, which is helping someone to look inward, outward, and forward, a highly effective leader can then focus their own development. Their own coaching development can focus on five specific skills:

1. Creating trust and an open dialogue
2. The use of great questions
3. Active listening or listening to influence
4. The act of giving motivating feedback
5. Creating a development plan

We can apply these five skills to enhance our general leadership effectiveness and specifically, to become a great coach. We cannot coach without a clear set of pipes and wiring between ourselves and the persons we are coaching. The ability to create trust and to have people run toward you with their problems rather than run away from you is a critical skill to develop as a coach. How does one gain trust? Highly disciplined and effective leaders first demonstrate vulnerability. Second, they are trustworthy themselves. Finally, they are more interested in others' development over their own success. As a coach I have found that developing these three specific attributes enables one to create an open dialogue and a trusting relationship, which will enable a broader coaching relationship.

Have you ever seen a wise, sagely leader? The person who is usually the least boisterous and asks the exact right question at the exact right time, bringing the meeting to a different place? This level of coaching is an art form, and this discipline is a lifelong journey. One simple technique to improve your ability to ask the right questions is to simply challenge yourself to replace all periods with question marks in your sentences. A second is to be intellectually and emotionally curious about the state of others over the need to express yourself. By being somewhat detached we can formulate what, how, when, and where questions to truly seek to help the person hear themselves out loud, and for us to truly understand. When I can seek to understand and enable the person to hear their own voice, I can get to that place where listening can begin.

There are many things to consider when being a great, active listener. A great coach allows others in the room to express themselves. An active listener reflects back, uses eyes, body, and hands, as well as pace and volume of speech to communicate understanding and to influence an emotional interchange with the person being coached. There are many ways to actively listen. I actually think listening is one of the great disciplines of great leaders. Active listening requires high levels of emotional intelligence and a selflessness that allows others to gain insight and challenge themselves.

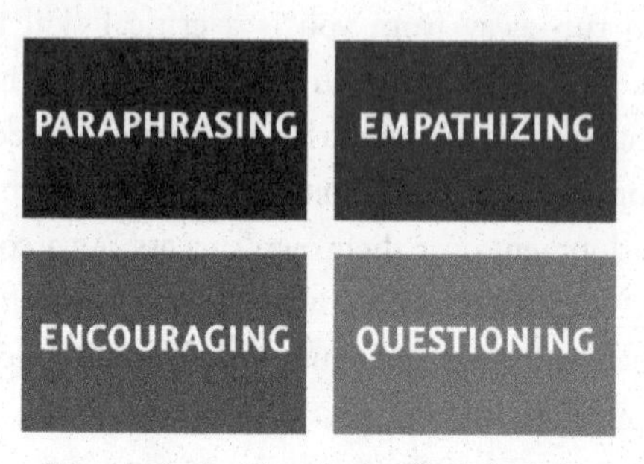

Figure 7. Active Listening Feedback Qualities

Perhaps the biggest skill to be developed to become a great coach is comfort with giving feedback. I find that self-soothing leaders who are uncomfortable giving feedback are ego-driven.

They want to make themselves comfortable over giving someone else the gift of feedback. Feedback is a gift.

Highly effective coaches have the ability to deliver while keeping the motivation in the other high. Giving feedback following a model like the SBI Model below, or the CAR Model that we'll discuss later, can be very helpful. These models enable a person to practice the act of giving feedback. I find great leaders who practice giving feedback are just as comfortable and practice asking for smart, critical feedback. The highly effective coach considers feedback a two-way dialogue, where a person can hear from you something that other leaders have not had the courage to give. Giving feedback following some framework allows you to have comfort and confidence, rather than relying on an ability to simply have a conversation. A coach has a large toolkit with multiple frameworks for giving feedback. Ask yourself this question: Do you have even one framework or model to give feedback to another person?

Let's take a look at the SBI Model:

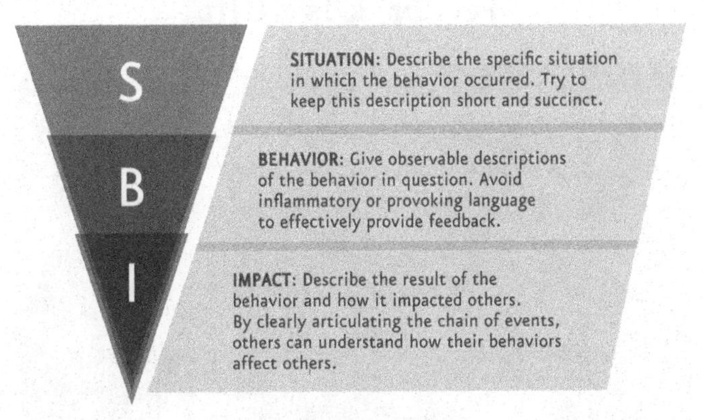

Figure 8. The SBI Model

Asking a question to clarify the situation gets you quick agreement on the context and allows the person to get comfortable with the direction of the conversation. Asking a question using a nice statement seeks to understand the behavior that is being observed and invites the other person to look at their own behavior. It is a critical part of the SBI Model. And whether positive or negative, offering someone to consider the impact or the implication of the behavior on the broader team and organization often gives weight to the feedback. A true coach who is practiced and disciplined doesn't consider feedback positive or negative. Feedback just is. A great coach and a highly effective leader above all is adept at feedback, both giving and receiving.

The final skill applied to our coaching model would be the act of preparing a development plan. I don't mean the human resources process for development planning. I mean the thrice annual conversation where we contract with persons who we're coaching, encouraging them to work on a specific behavior that has immediacy for the job and more importantly, immediacy for the person's career.

Feedback Is a Gift

I find many leaders are not adept at giving feedback. By following the SBI Model and using questions, feedback can become a superpower. Feedback is always a gift. Withholding that gift can be cruel. Even giving feedback sloppily, when coming from a place of caring and constructive concern, will always be a gift.

I had an employee named Jim and Jim had a temper. I got indirect feedback from colleagues that Jim was particularly aggressive in meetings that I did not attend. Now, indirect feedback is tricky in Jim's defense. So I thought about it a little bit and decided to take it on because if I withheld this feedback and allowed Jim to not be aware of how deeply his outburst had impacted his colleagues, ultimately it would hurt Jim as much as it would hurt the team. I approached Jim and simply said, "I understand last Thursday's meeting got a little heated, but I wasn't there. Could you walk me through the situation or walk me through your point of view as to what happened?" Jim explained that the meeting was heated and that everyone was using some coarse language.

Once Jim acknowledged the situation, I just shifted. I said, "Well Jim, is there a particular behavior in that meeting that you would want to redo?" Jim began to tell me about his three colleagues and what they said and did, so I paused, put my hand up gently, took a breath and said, "Jim, that's interesting and I am interested in that, but the specific question I asked is about your behaviors. What do you think you would like to redo or have another shot at doing a little better?" Jim paused and said, "Well I guess I could have..." He acknowledged some of his own coarse language. I thanked him and acknowledged it takes courage to look at yourself but once he acknowledged his own behavior, I didn't need to stay there any longer. I transitioned again and said, "Jim, thank you very much for acknowledging that. I just want to highlight that you're a valuable part of the team, but sometimes when you use coarse language, the impact on a team is that it heightens others' emotions and defenses, and perhaps you would be more effective if you could not only not heighten, but even act to cool the meeting when it gets particularly emotional. Perhaps Jim, your emotions serve you quite well sometimes, but maybe not if you want to advance in your career."

I wanted him to not do anything, but just think about how his emotions both serve him and may not serve him as he seeks to advance his career. I offered a statement of support and invited follow up with me the very next time he felt overly emotional. No, it's not one and done. Oftentimes, we must come back and follow the framework, coming from a constructive place and continue to ask questions that can help. We need to focus on self-discovery, not only on what's best for them in their job today, but what might serve them in their career long term.

In summary, coaching is a primary skill to becoming a highly effective enterprise leader. One's ability to coach individuals and small groups, to challenge and change their behavior, enhances engagement and productivity. Being competent at it means having the models and the skills as well as the approach, and having the confidence and the willingness to engage others where previous leaders have not. These are the hallmarks of a great coach. Coaching is like golf: You're never perfect, you'll never make 18 birdies. Coaching is a discipline that requires daily practice. By following the world's most simple coaching model—looking inward, outward, and helping others to look forward[xv]—and by applying basic skills like building trust, asking the right questions, actively listening, giving feedback, and agreeing on specific targets with the people being coached, you are already far ahead of other leaders. If a leader in an organization wants to drive engagement and productivity, they must be able to challenge and change behaviors and attitudes.

PROCESS	CONTENT
Get a Coach	Define a coaching model that fits you
Confidently Coach where you have no Job Mastery	Practice offering supportive, constructive feedback
Challenge yourself to gain esteem from others' recognition and advancement	React less. Question and Listen more.
Coach a person NOT in the majority class (walk in their shoes)	Have a development plan and conversation with all of your A and B players once per quarter

CHAPTER 5

The Hard Discipline of Building GREAT Teams and Groups in Leading in an Organization

OUR JOURNEY THUS FAR toward great leadership has walked us through the discipline of introspection and self-awareness, the discipline of creating an environment for productivity and engagement, the discipline of influencing without power, and discipline to become a great coach. The discipline we will explore next is the discipline to build great teams and to truly understand group dynamics.

As we leave job mastery and journey toward becoming a great leader, we find that we practice our original occupation much less. We lead and facilitate groups and teams with more frequency than we practice our original occupation. I often wonder why all CEOs aren't required to take a basic course in group dynamics. Presumably, most of us hire talented people, but the challenge then becomes getting those people to fully engage in small groups as we know small groups and teams provide a multiplier of productivity and organizational performance. I am often asked in my work as an organizational psychologist what percentage of my work is actual strategy or leadership or change versus pure psychology when working with leadership teams. It is often not the talent gaps that create the environment where a team may miss its deadline or fall short of expectations. It's often the group dynamic and the leader's inability to work with the group dynamic in an effective way to build a high-performance team. To me this is a primary and fundamental leadership challenge in American business. As you're reading this book, you're likely a member of multiple teams inside of your organization. Do you ever wonder how to effect change toward the positive in any team? Have you ever been frustrated by not being able to have an impact on a group or team? This chapter will take a very specific and precise point of view as to how to lead teams toward high-performance. We will do this leveraging what I call "the LENS Model."

Team as a Noun and a Verb

A team is a group of people coming together presumably for a common purpose and with a common set of goals. Team members have some level of interdependence with one another. At some level, they must work together to achieve their mission or accomplish the goals. Without interdependence, we would call them a group. There are many types of teams inside an organization system. Some teams must operate like a hockey team where all members must know where each other stands in all cases and must be able to make no look passes to one another. Some teams operate like wrestling teams or swimming teams in that individual contribution can be sound, but interdependence is not so high. I make this distinction because many of us must clearly articulate the purpose, the goals, and the level of interdependence required to perform to exceed expectations. Hackman describes team performance as stability to meet or exceed external and internal expectations.[xvi] High-performing teams both perform at a high level and interact in a positive and engaging way and are highly productive to exceed expectations. When we say high-performing team we intend to describe the levels of both engagement and productivity within the team.

As a leader it's also helpful to think about team as a noun, and teaming as a verb. Why is this helpful? As a highly effective leader, I am accountable as the team leader to drive engagement and productivity. The team then is a place. It is a now. It becomes a forum for interaction and productivity. I must take care of that forum in very specific and precise ways to increase the team's inner workings. Oftentimes, leaders find the group dynamic in any team to be ambiguous or hard to impact. We will address this in specific terms in a moment.

Let's talk about "teaming" as a verb. Teaming as a verb requires some level of selflessness, vulnerability, and contribution toward an agreed-upon set of outcomes, even in the case where those outcomes supersede the need to create individual esteem or outcomes. Teaming is the ability to give oneself over to a group that can exceed expectations. This level of discipline is not how everybody wants to interact, as we can see in the performance of seal teams. Day one of SEAL training requires selflessness and SEALS in training are given feedback daily on how much they have contributed or taken away from the performance of the team, and the performance of the team supersedes all individual needs. I find that great leaders easily team, whether leading or following. While having the ability to team as a verb is critical to be an effective organizational member, this chapter will specifically focus on the team leader and the team as a noun.

We draw from well-established literature to put three models together into what I call the "LENS Model." I certainly did NOT invent lettuce, nor the plastic bag. However, someone figured out that by cleaning and putting lettuce in a plastic bag, they could increase the value for themselves and the customer. Like lettuce in a bag, I have put these models together in a similar way. On the left, we loosely see Hackman's fundamental conditions, in the middle we see the ever-popular evolutionary perspective of team development, and out to the right we find the Lencioni Model for team dysfunction.

But by putting these models to use, we develop three different lenses, or perspectives, allowing a leader to specifically diagnose where a team is dysfunctional and how to move that team toward more function. It's no accident that Patrick Lencioni only labeled his book "the five dysfunctions of a team." The idea there is that all groups of humans have dysfunction at some level. For a leader to understand us and then have a specific lens to identify the dysfunction enables the leader to intervene and increase the performance and productivity of the team. I have been developing this LENS Model for decades now and I believe it to be a critical skill for all highly effective leaders, given that we work in groups and teams the majority of our careers.

The LENS Model

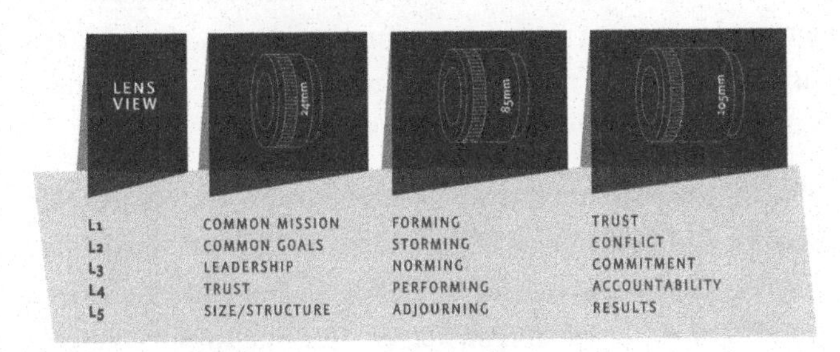

Figure 9. The LENS Model by Patrick Lencioni[xvii]

The LENS Model is meant to work in three columns, from left to right and top to bottom. The first column on the left is the fundamentals column, where most leaders miss the boat. Using the evolutionary perspective, a team is a group of living breathing human beings and like any group of living beings, it follows a lifecycle. In the fundamentals column, we can think of elementary school where one must matriculate to earn the right to go to high school. I find the middle column to be high school. Once we have completed the fundamentals analysis, we then move on. The third column to the right is the university model. Finally, Lencioni, who studied intact teams, gives us yet another lens to diagnose and develop team performance. Let's explore each column using our lens in a bit of detail.

Fundamentals

Over the years I have been asked to design what HR leaders referred to as team-building sessions. I have worked with hundreds of intact teams dealing with some level of dysfunction. My effort involved quickly assessing the team's specific dysfunction so that I could have a high impact on the team's performance. I have found that the fundamentals lens is most often a primary source of dysfunction. Leaders understanding the fundamentals lens can quickly assess what is missing or what dysfunction is present.

The first fundamental is a common purpose or mission. The second fundamental is a common set of team goals. The third is adjusted leadership. The fourth fundamental is trust and the fifth is size and structure. Imagine for a minute we had a team with eight members, we approached each of the eight members individually and asked one simple question? What does this team exist to do? When we begin to hear the variety of responses in language and in real difference, we may begin to see dysfunction. Think about it this way: What is the purpose or the mission of the New York Yankees? That's right—to win the World Series every year. Now ask, what is the mission or purpose of the San Diego Padres? It is not to win the World Series each and every year. In fact, it is most likely to field a competitive product and be a great member of the San Diego community. Our purpose guides us. Where the individual members may have a different sense of purpose, one can easily see dysfunction. This is a way to apply the LENS Model in a fundamental way to identify if mission or purpose is in fact okay, missing, or not aligned, causing dysfunction. We can take this same approach with all five fundamentals.

The place where I find the most dysfunction is in the team's alignment around common goals. In the story below, I share a real example of how the team's common goals are a primary source of team dysfunction.

It's a Mission, or It's a Mess

I often get called in to work with teams at various places on their functional performance. In one particular case, working with a very large public company, the head of HR asked me to work directly with the executive team at an offsite, as her CEO was not pleased with how the team had been behaving and functioning with one another. I asked if I could interview the team members in advance of putting together an agenda and facilitating the event and she said yes. I have a series of interview questions that follow along the LENS Model, in particular assessing the fundamentals that we talk about.

So I asked the CEO if the team had a common set of goals and the CEO said, "Well of course we do. We work on all of the goals of the organization." During my next interview, which was about a half-hour after this, I asked the CFO if the team had a common set of goals, and he said, "No, not that I know. I mean, I have my goals. I know they have their goals, but I don't think we have anything like team goals." My very next meeting was with the COO and I asked if the team had a common set of goals and he said, "We used to, but I'm not sure what they are anymore. Maybe we should set them offsite." Who's wrong or right? Who has a better view than the others? Clearly, this is dysfunctional. How can three members of the senior-most team in the organization have such different views? This is not acceptable. Any high-performing team would have a manageable set of six or eight interdependent goals by which they're driving value and managing risk in the enterprise.

This is particularly true in the case of a senior executive team. If you think about the very fundamental conditions by which high-performing teams exist, two of their very basics are a common mission and a common set of team goals that drive team performance. Without these two fundamental conditions, you see other things pop up as symptoms, but they're truly symptoms. The root cause is the lack of common goals. Symptoms may look like the lack of appropriate leadership, low trust, or inappropriate or absent conflict. These things often exist because the "what" isn't right. The "what" is the common mission and the common goals. Then the "how" comes into play. The "how" will let trust evolve. These fundamental conditions were missing. This was a very large public company and we were seeing all sorts of dysfunction that sprung from that root cause. As we cleaned that up, we clarified what the CEO wanted. The CEO naturally started the discussions with questions like, "Then, how will we handle account Y?" and these became much more productive conversations. I often get too much credit for simply highlighting the fundamentals of group dynamics and team performance. It's my belief that all senior leaders, as they ascend, do less of their functional expertise and more of leading experts in the form of teams and groups. If I had one wish, it would be that all CEOs would become experts at big group dynamics and how to build high performing teams.

The third fundamental is what I call adjusted leadership. It turns out that Deming's TQM idea of leaderless groups with cross functional expertise being able to perform at a high level was absolutely wrong. Fortunately or unfortunately, the data is in and we have found that groups of humans need leadership. When I say that, what I mean is teams need a leader who is astute enough to adjust their leadership style to meet the team where it is and help develop the team toward high performance. As an example, a team in a transition or turnaround state may require a level of toughness and organizational design expertise that one may not need when a leader first encounters, for example, an existing high-performing team. In the latter case, motivating, inspiring, and challenging may be required as a primary leadership set of skills. Adjusted leadership means the leader assesses the team and delivers the kind of leadership that enables high-performance.

The fourth fundamental is trust. According to the work motivation, it is difficult for a human to fully engage and extend one's effort without feeling a sense of being trusted. Leaders develop the discipline of building trust not as a soft skill but as a fundamental imperative to drive high-performing teams. Trust is not an emotion. Trust is the aggregated outcome of a series of interactions that tell somebody how vulnerable he or she may be, how much they should share, and how much they are willing to be selfless and reliant upon others. The ineffective leader will focus on the hub and spoke model or top-down trust, where the respected leader develops trust with each member. While this is required and very fundamental, what I have found is that leaders can create an environment for team members to trust one another and their leaders to create a level of accountability and trust where peers can maintain relationships with each other. The leadership discipline requires an environment that demands norms be enforced. When we look at exceptionally high performing teams, we find trust and accountability, where team members hold themselves to a high standard, calling themselves out in front of the group where shortcomings occur, where members no longer even have to hold one another accountable; rather, the individuals hold themselves accountable. I find in these environments trust goes up exponentially, which allows for engagement to follow and ultimately leads to productivity. Trust is fundamental for motivation and engagement, and motivation and engagement are key precursors to meeting and exceeding expected outcomes.

The fifth fundamental that we can examine through the LENS Model—and the most overlooked, particularly in corporate settings—is size and structure. In our efforts to be inclusive, we often complicate teams by adding too many humans. When sizing a team, we often think of required membership first, and about diversity of membership from a skill standpoint or even functional standpoint last. This is obviously a mistake based upon the mission and goals of the team. We want to start with trait diversity so that we bring the traits required to accomplish the mission and goals, and then secondly, think about functional or occupational diversity.

This discipline is nonobvious and often overlooked in our effort to be inclusive and fair. Being inclusive and fair is critically important, but we need to do it from the perspective of trait diversity mapped to the mission and goals. When I speak of structure, I speak of formal and informal structure. From a formal standpoint, how do we define leadership? Have we defined how information will flow, how decisions will be made, and where the requisite authority will be? When I think of informal structure, I think about how the work really gets done in a team. Does one member take all of the administrivia or is one member the hero and takes the credit? When I think of size and structure, it is fundamental that I consider the basics of how work gets done,

Taking our lens and looking at five fundamentals of high-performing teams allows us as leaders to specifically assess areas of gap or dysfunction so that we can specifically put an action plan in place to improve team performance. You can almost do without the other two columns in the model because most dysfunction occurs at a very fundamental level. But for the sake of building highly effective leaders, let's take a look at using the LENS Model on the other two columns.

Evolution

In the second column, we see the model originally asserted by Bruce Tuckman (1965). The model says that groups of humans initially form, storm, norm, perform and adjourn. For some reason, this basic model is not well known or forgotten by high-performing team leaders and team leaders across the board. The classic mistake is that the leader says, "Okay, you're all here, you're all on board, let's perform… go." And then, for some reason, performance is expected. This model reminds us that groups of humans cannot perform until they work through a maturational or evolutionary set of phases. This model reminds us that when we bring groups of humans together, we should allow debate during storming. and not until the phase is resolved can the team establish norms and get to high-performance. The active leader works early and often. This is a classic mistake made from the perspective of common sense. Leadership is not always about common sense; this is one example. The leader may try to harmonize and avoid discord or debate, but in fact, that is retarding the development of the team. And, it may be limiting the team's ability to ever be high-performing. The leader in the storming phase needs to understand the model to know how storming is to occur. That is the leader who can build high-performing teams.

How does one facilitate storming? One must have the courage and modeling knowledge to pass these measurable, aligned, relevant, critical questions. These critical discussion questions are meant to spark debate and must occur in the group so then when members start to disagree and debate, the leader can enforce the rules of engagement. When the team sees that it is acceptable and even expected to disagree, they may be ready to do it in a safe and respectful way. In so doing, they will bring forward differences that are usually, largely unstated. Remember people may often disagree or question, but they just don't say it, which typically is labeled as passive-aggressive behavior, as members express discord in private. The exercise of asking the smart, critical questions in the group models the behavior that discord is not only okay, but it's encouraged. The leader does not get involved in the content of the discussion, rather moderates the process of the debate. In doing this, the leader's discipline will enable the evolution from storming to norming.

As a leader, one does not just expect people to accept their roles easily. Role clarity—or the lack thereof—is often a form of resistance, not confusion. The leader who handles these questions as resistance gets high performance. Role clarity, handoffs, and transitions—where do I stop and where do I start?—is a critical activity as we leave storming and get people to perform. A classic example of this is the Los Angeles Lakers with Kobe Bryant and Shaquille O'Neal. Kobe lacked trust in Shaq to do the work of the center. In doing so, he endangered himself and hurt the team by being out of position. Norming allows people to align their talents and skills to a specific set of tasks. Without notifying the rest of the team, the team's performance will be hurt.

Leaders must be aware that when they have a team that is performing at a high level, then the leader's is not to simply maintain it or lock it into place. That is the fool's error. Rather, the discipline of the leader with a high-performing team is to find places where excess capacity might exist in the team, so the team can, in fact, give more. Or, with the team performing at a high level, the leader can have a window to view where the team could use further improvement.

So, as a leader developing the discipline of building high-performance teams, you must look at the five fundamentals to seek to fill gaps or make improvements. By identifying where a team is and understanding how to move toward higher performance, the leader can positively impact the group and the members' lives and careers.

A final note on the model. Adjournment happens only when the mission is accomplished or membership, even one, changes. In this way, building a high-performing team is an ongoing process, as teams are always evolving and changing. Teams who stay in place for too long, by the very nature of time, may see their performance go down. Leaders who can manage teams through many missions and many goals without changing membership are high performers and should be sought out. But changing goals and changing membership and changing environments are a fact of life. Team leadership, now using the LENS Model, is critical, along with teaming as a verb. Knowing how to engage as a leader and a follower is a discipline of a highly effective leader.

Lencioni

The final column—or what I call the college or university level—is where I use the LENS Model[xviii] to identify dysfunction. Function was given to us by Patrick Lencioni. Lencioni's work reminds us that all teams are built on trust. The extent to which we trust will be a corollary to the extent that we experience. Where we had an absence of trust, we may see an absence of conflict. The consequence of that is that team goals may go down. Remember humans are social creatures who are always committed to something. Our goal is to use the LENS Model to identify the level of trust and get the right level of conflict, or storming, to enable commitment to be as high as possible. You can best see this when trying to hold someone accountable who is not committed. When we have high commitment to team goals, people will subjugate themselves and allow themselves to be held accountable.

The LENS Model as a Discipline

I often find teams within corporate organizations to be at many different places when I look at the LENS Model. I like to use the LENS Model and I encourage leaders to develop discipline using it to identify the biggest challenges or gaps that would immediately increase team performance. I find that when leaders work with teams in a positive direction, allowing for engagement and productivity, the leader changes, becoming a highly-effective leader. A trustful or soft skill approach is needed. Leading teams to higher performance takes discipline and intellect. Knowing the LENS Model is one aspect; putting the LENS Model into practice is a whole other. Many leaders have multiple teams and groups. Leading their members to have specific practice in applying the LENS Model and trying different techniques is the work and discipline of the highly-effective leader.

Leaders must first use the LENS Model to assess where their teams are currently, to identify a problem or where the gaps are. The leader can then develop specifics in putting together development actions. For example, we may find a team stuck at "storming." In this case, we use the model to assess, and we may intentionally facilitate a discussion leveraging the specific critical questions about role clarity, resources, or other barriers to full performance. Presumably, the unstated then gets stated and members can come to new agreements.

Leadership acumen and leadership discipline are often expressed when leading teams in the form of a meeting. Most ineffective leaders define meetings as administrative chores or tasks. The highly effective leader defines a meeting as a gathering of well-intended people who are attempting to accomplish many goals while under-resourced. The discipline of conducting effective meetings as a leader is often overlooked as a meaningful leadership activity. Yet a meeting is a forum or group of humans who have opinions and have emotional interactions with you and other people in the organization. Meetings are a tool to communicate and make decisions for groups and teams.

Meetings

Why will we discuss meetings? It's quite simple: meetings are a primary method to interact with a team. The disciplined leader sees a meeting as an opportunity to take time for groups of people to communicate or make decisions. The problem is that meetings have generally become ineffective, defined as an administrative task, and worse yet, we have become mental slaves to the one-hour time slot.

The one-hour time slot is an artifact from the software scheduling systems and/or an artifact from some early boss. The one-hour meeting in and of itself is arbitrary. Because of this, meetings—and the time they waste—are an epidemic in all organizations. Since the one-hour time slot for most meetings is arbitrary, the highly disciplined and effective leader never pays attention to the one-hour time slot, but rather builds the agenda and the information to be shared from the bottom up.

Parkinson's law reminds us that if we give a group of humans a time to complete a task, they will take all of that time. This is why the one-hour average meeting is maddening. In many cases, the effective, disciplined leader could cut the one hour to 30 minutes. In so doing, they increase the urgency to be on time, they improve the words and interactions, and increase the discipline to stick to the agenda.

The second problem with meetings, other than taking an inordinate amount of time away from people's productivity, is that they take time away from people's family. Let me explain. When a well-intended person leaves four or five meetings on a given Tuesday, they find themselves doing their work at home, or returning email after 5 PM. They're doing this because we kept them away from full productivity and put them in meeting spaces. Because they're well intended, they still want to complete their work, while trying to avoid telephone calls from their significant others. Well intended people will take time from their families to do their real work because we as leaders have wasted their time in unproductive meetings.

A third problem that is very difficult for many people to understand is the cost of poorly run meetings. I as a leader understand the amount of time I'm going to spend is the cost in labor hours of the members in the meeting. I can easily do that estimated calculation—for example, 8 people at $200 per hour for one hour. Is the information to be shared at the meeting or the decisions to be made worth $1600? If it is, I'll have the meeting. If it isn't, I'll find a different forum or means to have the information exchange or the decision made, because when I'm holding that amount of cost in a meeting once a week for

52 weeks, that $1600 multiplied by 50 is a far greater number. It is funny that people who take great pride in efficiency still run poor meetings, driving a high soft cost to the organization. In summary, meetings are not administrative tasks. They're an opportunity to enforce high performance teams by enabling information to be shared in an exciting and engaging way. Meetings can be less than one hour with increased productivity, increased work-life balance, and increased efficiency, which all deliver cost benefits back to our organization. The lazy leader defaults to the one-hour time space and allows the group to use the full time or more. A disciplined, practiced leader is endeavoring to get better at gauging teams and recognizing the space it needs.

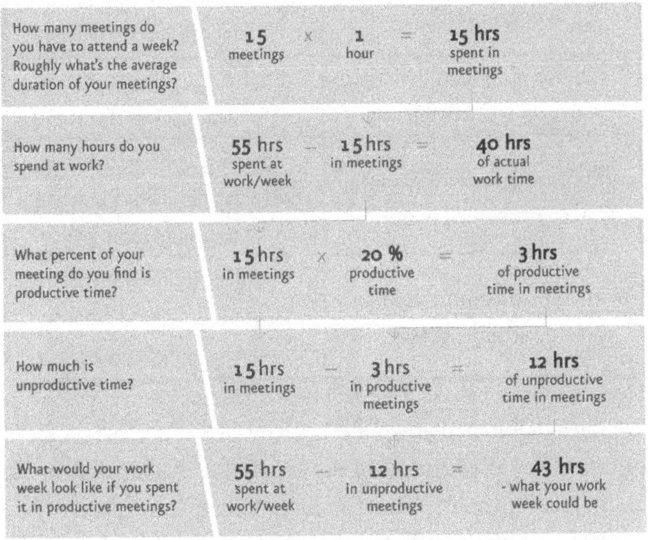

How many meetings do you have to attend a week? Roughly what's the average duration of your meetings?	15 meetings	×	1 hour	=	15 hrs spent in meetings
How many hours do you spend at work?	55 hrs spent at work/week	–	15 hrs in meetings	=	40 hrs of actual work time
What percent of your meeting do you find is productive time?	15 hrs in meetings	×	20 % productive time	=	3 hrs of productive time in meetings
How much is unproductive time?	15 hrs in meetings	–	3 hrs in productive meetings	=	12 hrs of unproductive time in meetings
What would your work week look like if you spent it in productive meetings?	55 hrs spent at work/week	–	12 hrs in unproductive meetings	=	43 hrs - what your work week could be

Figure 10. A Model for Time Wasted in Meetings

While coaching is a superpower, understanding and specifically using the LENS Model with high-performing teams is a practice and a discipline that will increase the engagement and productivity of the groups and teams you lead and are a part of. The LENS Model moves us from an amorphous group or team to a precise view of where function and dysfunction occur so the leader can intervene appropriately. The discipline of driving team performance is a constant pursuit of the highly-effective leader, and a place where productivity has a multiplier. Highly-engaged humans can accomplish far greater things than any individual. The leader's ability to understand the dynamics of high-performing teams is foundational to enterprise leadership and unique among leaders across organizations.

PROCESS	CONTENT
What are your weaknesses as a team member	Use the LENS Model to diagnose where one of your teams are stuck
Seek to gain feedback on yourself as a team leader	Name all of the teams in your leadership purview
Have you studied group dynamics and teams	Have a specific Team Development Plan for your primary teams
Can you care about the team over a single player	Be verbal about the team behaviors that are acceptable, and not

We started this chapter wondering why all CEOs aren't required to take a basic course in group dynamics. Presumably, most of us hire talented people, then put them into groups and expect a multiplier effect on productivity and organizational performance. It is very rare that the actual talent within the team causes the team to miss its deadline or to fall short of expectations. It's often the result of the group dynamic and the leader's inability to work with the group dynamic in an effective way to build a high-performance team and enable that team to meet or exceed the expectations of all stakeholders. I find very few leaders actually even know of the fundamental conditions that must exist for a team to perform. This chapter was intended to close that gap and more as it relates to building high performance teams.

CHAPTER 6

The Discipline of Strategic Thinking

WE'VE ALREADY WALKED through the disciplines of introspection and self-awareness, the discipline of creating an environment, the discipline of influencing without power, and the discipline to become a great coach. And in Chapter 5, we discussed the discipline to build great teams and to truly understand group dynamics. And as we leave job or occupational mastery and journey toward being a great leader, we find that we actually begin to think differently. Let's explore strategic thinking as a discipline we must work to master.

Among the primary reasons I wrote this book was to seek the answers to questions that Jim Collins posed.[xix] How does one become a Level V leader? It occurs to me that leaders with great self-awareness have great followership. We've also explored how leaders who create an environment that's engaging and can influence rather than use power get the most out of their talent, and build great teams. Those leaders would be working in the direction of Level V leadership. Level V leadership as defined by leadership effectiveness, whether the leader is present or not. The sixth discipline we will explore to close that gap and become a highly functioning executive leader in any corporation or organization is the discipline of strategic thinking. We will cover the ability to move beyond today and consider the implications of our choices and decisions and our actions into the future, where they impact true value.

Strategic Thinking…what is that? What does it mean, and how is it demonstrated? It may be, at times, coded language for, "You're not in the cool kid club." It turns out when we ask people who make promotion decisions, "What is strategic thinking?" we don't get a clear answer, like we do, for example, with being a great coach, which can be evidenced by having "ready-now successors." So with ready-now successors, we know that's real. We get aligned and cogent input, and we can study it and change it and watch it work. When we start using words like strategic thinking, we get a wide array of what that actually means, and sometimes it's actually coded language to keep people out of the C-suite.

A Strategic View is More Complete

Upon concluding a couple months of a strategic planning initiative with a combined group of board members and C-Suite executives, there were a series of final presentations with key strategic decisions to be dispositioned. The key question with a month plus of analysis was "Should we expand our footprint into Latin America?" The market opportunity, market conditions, and growth potential were clearly in the right direction, and the group gained momentum around, "Yes, we should." As we began to dive into some of the how-to's and what-for's, there were debates about how best to do it, when and how to budget, etc. There was a very wise board member who sat in the back corner and said very little, but she raised her hand to ask a question of the CEO. The question was this: "Who will lead the operation in this Central American country?" The CEO quickly worked to have an answer, which was clearly the wrong thing to do, and he said, "Jim, our superstar CEO will lead the effort for the first year until we find a leader." The room went silent. It got very awkward. What this board member had done in her wisdom was ask a strategic question. It looked simple. It didn't look very strategic, but it was very strategic.

The room went silent and it got awkward because everyone knew this question couldn't be answered at the moment and the answer given was the wrong answer. The gathered executives and their team members heard the question and that awkward silence was, "Oh, how can we extend this executive from California who doesn't speak the language and know the culture and lead the first year—the most critical year of an expansion—into a foreign market?" The CEO then went on with the meeting. The board member pushed me and the CEO after the meeting, asking if she could have a moment with us. She didn't say the answer was the wrong answer. She simply asked the CEO to weigh the pros and cons and the implications of having a non-local leader in this critical time in this critical position. She asked that he reconsider his decision. So, strategic thinking doesn't have to be complex, but it does have to be out into the future, balancing value, relevance, and risk right along with key strategic decisions on who will lead in a new venture in a foreign market. Other considerations must be included. Business literature is littered with errors that are primarily driven by tactical thinking in a strategic space. Strategic thinkers employ a forward-view of value, relevance, and risk. There are many, many frameworks available to help them.

The reason I'm bringing up this point is because it is important as a leader that we realize this is the second-most frequently reported answer to the question of why people don't get promoted. But it doesn't have a clear, cogent meaning and it frustrates HR people. It frustrates smart people. Let's unpack what strategic thinking can and does mean so that leaders of all types may develop those strategic thinking skills, enabling career and leadership growth and development.

I have found that, analogous to emotional intelligence, strategic thinking is a learnable set of skills. Strategic thinking skills are critical to leadership effectiveness and appear to be the ability to look out into the future, and to look from the external environment to the internal environment. Second, strategic thinking involves the ability to take a holistic view of value, relevance, and risk in decision-making. And third, it includes the ability to think systemically. This may include scenario planning or thinking from the perspective of the 7S framework initially asserted by McKinsey.[xx] Finally, strategic thinking leads to integration over replication. If you think about it, these ways of thinking could answer the question that Jim Collins posed as we think about ascending to Level V leadership. Collins talked about great Level IV and V leaders having disciplined thinking. Being disciplined and thinking strategically are analogous.

Let's explore four specific strategic thinking techniques, and learn the skills needed to enhance our discipline around strategic thinking.

First, when evaluating a situation or thinking about decisions, I would like to assert future and outside-oriented thinking does not happen naturally, but rather, it's a disciplined form of thinking. I'd like to describe a 3-, 12-, and 24-month model. That is, when I evaluate a situation or make a decision, I will want to think about the implications 3 months out, 12 months out, and 24 months out. This is an easily learnable skill that can help one make more holistic and disciplined decisions.

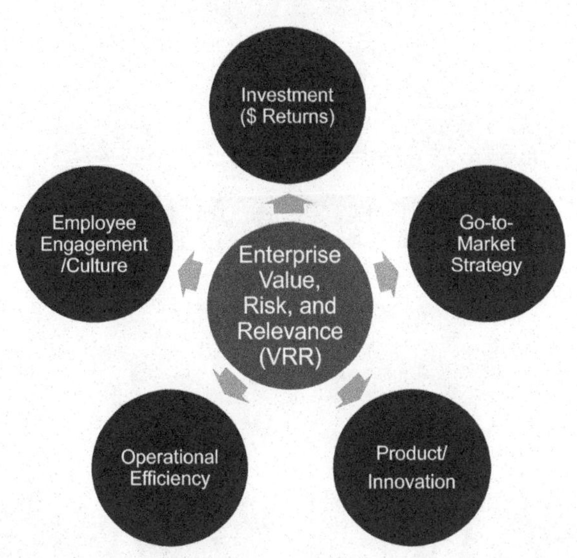

Figure 11. The Value, Risk, and Relevance Model

Second, when leveraging the Value, Risk, and Relevance Model, we need to view the Value part of the model as a "spinning triangle" for developing a strategic mind-set. Let's look at Value. We need to expand the decision-making from just an operational point of view—or even just a shareholder point of view of value—to value for the customer, employee, and the shareholder at the same time. Value defined is the worth in monetary terms of the technical, economic, service, and social benefits a customer / company receives in exchange for the price it pays for a market offering.

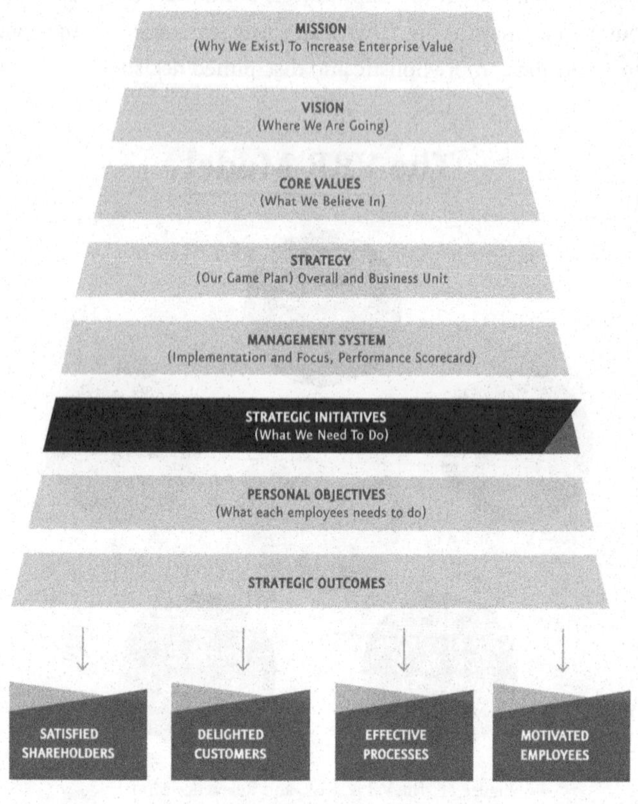

Figure 12. Executing On Your Mission

Then, can one balance value decisions with risk, or downside implications. I have observed risk factors can get ignored or minimized for ease and comfort (convenience), and then observed exuberance not offset with plans to mitigate risks. This lack of full consideration of risk comes from both ease and comfort and the need to "not be viewed as negative." One can explore risks through questioning and brainstorming. Techniques like SWOT or Barrier Analysis can offer an objective view to assess risk and allow you as the leader to be the "adult in the room."

We also need to consider relevance. Whether we are gaining value or mitigating risk, will our portfolio, product, or service maintain relevant to key customer segments into the future? By expanding from a simple view of shareholder value to the VRR Model, one can develop a strategic perspective using this disciplined framework.

Third, systems thinking. Systems thinking takes many forms. In its most basic definition, it is thinking about any one variable existing in an ecosystem of other variables, where the variables are dependent upon one another. Scenario planning, or the ability to think of multiple scenarios, their probability of occurrence, and their business impact is a simple and disciplined way of thinking strategically.

Another example of systems thinking is to use the 7S framework, whereby any strategic choice or decision exists in a system and is impacted by structure, skills, systems, and shared values. Systems thinking is a way to broaden one's thinking in a specific and disciplined way. This skill forces us to think of multiple implications to our scenarios and decision making, thus opening up our field of consideration.

Fourth, strategic thinking requires integrating past experiences with new learning and new stimuli. The term "learning agility" has become popular of late. It basically means to express one's ability to take in new information and apply it to present situations where decisions are made. One's ability to learn and grow may in fact slightly decline as we age and the motivation to challenge yourself to integrate rather than to replicate takes great discipline. It is true that our brains become a bit less facile after about the mid-30s and learning does require a little more effort and attention. This is why this discipline is so important. Learning agility is the discipline to begin to integrate rather than replicate.

Two additional concepts will help us understand the idea of learning agility: mindsets and replication.

Mindsets. A "fixed mindset," proposed by Stanford professor Carol Dweck in her book *Mindset*,[xxi] describes people who see their qualities as fixed traits that cannot change. She also proposed a "growth mindset," which describes people who believe their success depends on time and effort. People with a growth mindset feel their skills and intelligence can be improved with effort and persistence. They learn from failure. A growth mindset is a movement toward strategic thinking in that it implies one is never finished thinking, as the world is always changing. Therefore, we must always be integrating "new" ideas, realities and constructs. The opposite of a growth mindset is replication.

Replication. It is easy to look at a new situation and apply old learning or experience to that situation to figure out the right path forward. However, this is a flawed and a non-strategic way of thinking, and even a lazy way of thinking. It's not possible that today's decisions and challenges can solely be addressed using our past experiences, memories, and old information.

The world is changing rapidly and while your experiences can and should inform your thinking, it is not the place to stop.

When I use the term integrating, what I mean is the ability to apply new methods, criteria, and points of view to a situation, as well as pulling from past experiences and memories to think more holistically about a given situation, person, or decision. Integrating requires being up to date on new thinking techniques, decision-making models, and using strategic questions as focal points to engage bright and talented people around you, as a leader would. Strategic thinking in its most basic form ought not be done alone, and is a great opportunity to engage followers and demonstrate leadership. The insecure leader has to have the right answer. The vulnerable and secure later wants the best answer.

Nardelli's Formula for Failure

The story of Robert Nardelli is pretty well known. Nardelli is a famous replicator—as many leaders are—rather than being an integrator. Nardelli was passed over for the CEO job 30 years ago at GE. When he left and landed at The Home Depot, he saw a retail business that was pretty undisciplined and lazy. He brought in his people from GE, brought in GE methods, and he thought if he could GE-ize Home Depot, performance would go up. He did not integrate the consumer part of the business, the branded parts of the business, and in fact even considered retail as being on par with manufacturing. His tenure at Home Depot saw about a 6% rise in enterprise value. The problem was that Lowes went up almost 200%. Nardelli was a replicator seeking to replicate his wonderful career at GE into a new environment without integrating new information, new talent, and new data. Nardelli then went on to Chrysler, also a manufacturing business like GE, and he tried to GE-ize Chrysler. Obviously, his tenure at Chrysler is well-known. He did a lot of damage to the company's value and caused a mass loss of jobs. We find leaders all over who used terms that tell us exactly what they intend to do. "Well, at my previous company we did this," or, "in my experience..." This work experience is great, but it's even better when we take in new data and new information and allow new talent to challenge us. Lookout for replicators; they create a lot of damage. We want to leverage our experience and integrate new information as a learning leader.

PROCESS	CONTENT
The discipline to move past your first thought or reaction	The use of a future-oriented questions
The maturity to pose a question rather than take a position	The expansion of value out into the future and for whom
Have you been strategic at any point in your life and how has that worked	The practice of systems thinking to evaluate strategic questions
The courage to be willing to be work, as strategic choices require leadership courage	The 7S practice of seeing the impact of a strategic decision on other organization elements

In summary, there are two reasons well-intended and smart leaders may not develop or advance in their career. Those reasons are the lack of a ready successor, and the real or perceived lack of strategic thinking. Coaching is the recipe for the ready successor. There may not be an easily-translated formula for strategic thinking because in some cases, it can be coded language to enable certain types of people to ascend to senior leadership positions. But, it has been my experience that by driving your own disciplined strategic thinking techniques, you can become the adult in the room or on the stage when evaluating situations and making decisions.

Strategic thinking can be developed and is critical as one ascends in their career. Strategic thinking is a core leadership discipline that enables bright and talented people, new innovative techniques, and disciplined activities and methods to be leveraged as a leadership set of tools to get the best possible outcomes. Tactical decisions often don't require leadership attention and are best handled through delegation, which enables and empowers those around you. Strategic situations, decisions, planning, and/or strategic thinking are the realm of the Level V leader. These skills are learnable, tangible and a constant area of focus for the developing leader.

CHAPTER 7

The Discipline of Being a Change Leader

AS WE LEAVE job or occupational mastery and journey toward being a strategic thinker, we must explore the counter-intuitive and critical role you will play as a change leader. Think about that term in a basic way. Your role in today's business environment is not just to think about the changes required to create value, relevance, and offset risk, but to then put plans in place, and FINALLY—and this is the place where most leaders fall short—actually lead humans through change. As we have seen through the pandemic, global disruption in information security and the ever increasing rate of innovation, change and the ability to lead change is a critical discipline to be developed.

There are actually two ways to think about leading humans through change. One can think about change as being thrust upon us. We may see our need as leaders to react quickly and lead people through change as something that's being done to us. This chapter speaks a little bit more about change being driven by dynamic leaders and a dynamic organization and industry and environment, where one is actually driving continuous improvement constantly. In either case, one's ability to meet humans through change is absolutely critical. Having the best idea and the best action plan is interesting but if I cannot get engagement, performance, and productivity out of individuals and teams, what good is the best idea and plan? In this chapter we will explore the why, what, and how as well as the 3A Model as a discipline to master as a change leader.

[2]

Definition of Change

So what is change? This word is thrown around a lot in today's business environment. Change represents any difference from the status quo. And while that may sound simple, as humans we have a need to conserve calories, to master our work, and to work in the most efficient way possible, add on to this that changing the status quo comes with elements of both crisis and opportunity. Any significant change that one can think of brings with it an element of danger and an element of opportunity. While many times the danger is obvious, sometimes the opportunity takes a long view to see. Think about the downsizing world. A well-intentioned leader loses

[2] Phonetically "Kiki," meaning "crisis, trouble."

her job. While this may seem like a crisis today, labor statistics clearly bear out that when people go through a transition, they often wind up with an increase in pay. In the labor market where unemployment of 5 percent or less exists, new opportunities come faster than one expects. So while the day of notification was a crisis, the opportunity that's presented at the same time may not be seen immediately. The disciplined leader understands that in all cases for herself as well as for her followers, change has both crisis and opportunity. And by leading from the mindset of both, and holding this paradox to be true, one is now prepared to lead change.

The mind-set of a change leader is critical. I assert the content that is critical to get one's mind-set right to lead change is the 3A Model:

Accountability

- Delegation
- Integrity and Trust
- Managerial Courage
- Standing Alone

Agility

- Comfortable Dealing with Ambiguity
- Future-Oriented
- Flexible and Adaptable

Attitude

- Perseverance
- Patience and Composure
- Approachability
- Self-Development

When we change we are challenging efficiency and conservation of the status quo. Now let's overlay how truly important our work is to us. One's occupation in our culture is a primary driver of the "esteem" (the force) and achievement in the ego. So now we start to see the problem. As a part of the human condition, we want to find routine and mastery. Secondly, one's occupation that we have mastery over gives us steam and achievement and even identity. In our culture what we do matters, so no matter how good a great change idea is, it is not the fault of the human when they resist; rather, it's a part of the human condition. We all resist when change is being done to us. We have greater probability of acceptance and engagement when we are part of the change thinking or early in the change process. But to be clear, no one is disrupted in something as important as their mastery of their occupation.

This begins to inform why change is difficult. In organizations we often talk about dozens, hundreds, or thousands of employees that have to be led through some change process. On top of that, there are many other changes going on inside of any organization or industry. Change leadership is among the most fundamental leadership disciplines. A leader can really distinguish themselves in their ability to lead change differently than others. Finally, change leadership is where common sense runs out of room and leadership, strategy, and complexity take over. In other words, things that seem obvious or driven by common sense are the wrong things to do in times of change. The classic example of this is illustrated in the box below.

Mindset + Typical Reaction + Leader Behaviors

In one year of my career I witnessed both of these examples. In one organization, while I was hired to help with change management, my client was notified by one of their largest customers that the customer was going to stop placing orders for this particular product from this particular distribution center in a particular part of the country. The CEO got on an airplane with me and a couple of his other executives and flew to the location. He called an all hands meeting but started like this:

"We got some news that in about 11 months this particular customer is going to stop placing orders for this product at this distribution center, which will cause this distribution center to be cut by 80 percent from a headcount perspective. I want you to know that we would like you all to stay and that things can change; however, you all have families, so for that reason, if you choose to quit today, you will be offered a full severance with outplacement services. If you choose to stay through to the end, you'll be paid a retention bonus with all of the same severance and same outplacement services that everyone else will get during the next nine months. We will open a Career Center so that you can learn to network and create a resume, and we will let you take hours off the floor for you to get trained so that you can gain full employment either between now and then or when the news comes that we may have to close this center. I care about you and I'll keep you informed if there are any changes."

A couple of months later, I was working with another client that was being acquired. When the acquisition was going to happen, there would be several points of redundancy in all of the G&A functions. The CEO called an all hands meeting and said, "Some of you have seen in the news that company X is trying to purchase us. It will be about 90 days between today and when the deal may close. I want you to know that as I see it, nothing will change. I don't think anything will impact you directly until after the close and even then, I don't suspect there'll be any changes."

In which of the above scenarios do you think the employees were more highly engaged and more productive? There's always change coming. Addressing change with a balanced perspective, in an honest fashion, with other well-intended adults may seem to be an obvious approach, but an awful lot of leaders forget this. In all change, there's crisis, and an opportunity to embrace both crisis and opportunity. The task for a leader is to drive up engagement and maintain some level of productivity. Everyone knows that when one company acquires another in the same space, there will be changes. Hope is never a plan and treating adults as if they're not adults is irresponsible.

Types of Change

Not all changes are created equal. There are Type I, Type II, and Type III changes, where Type III changes represent a paradigm shift in how people approach their work. As you can see from the arrow model, Type I changes require some degree of consistency, but are generally managed by local managers and teams. Type III changes require specific change leadership, understanding and change planning. For this segment, we will assume that change leadership will be applied in a disciplined way for Type II and Type III changes.

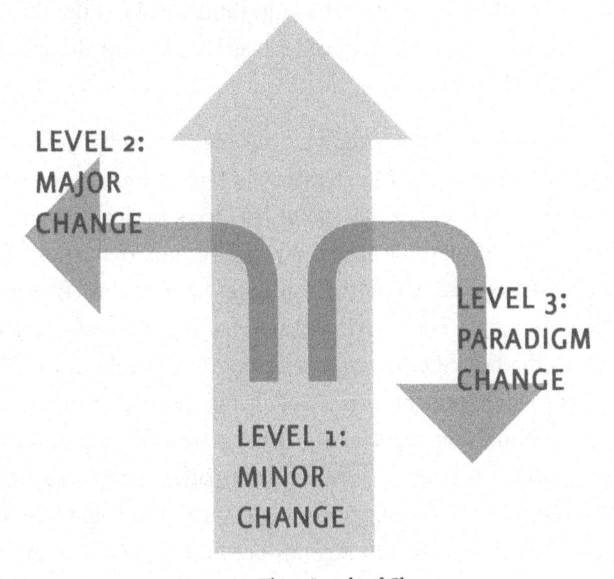

Figure 13. Three Levels of Change

Type II and Type III changes are typically evidenced in mergers or acquisitions, reductions in force, or large technology implementations. There are many other examples of these. When the literature talks about why change efforts fail, writers often forget to mention that the M&A occurred, but the value was lost—or, the technology was turned on but usage was low and rework and errors were high. So when we think about change efforts failing, it's not that the actual change didn't occur. The failure occurs by not getting people engaged and productive as quickly as possible. If we understand that the outcome of any good change in leadership is always the speed to get to normal or higher than normal productivity, as well as the speed to get to normal or higher than normal engagement. Simply put, a great change leader understands that speed is your friend, even at the cost of exact accuracy. Also simply put, any great change leader is trying to get the greatest engagement and productivity as quickly as possible. Once we have these fundamentals in place, we can begin thinking about the typical reaction to the change, as well as our leadership disciplines applied to those reactions.

Let's explore the second step for a disciplined leader to master when it comes to leading change: the typical human reaction to change. While I'm not going to account for individual differences, we have learned through group dynamics and organizational behavior that groups of humans typically follow the grief curve originally asserted by Elisabeth Kübler-Ross in the book *On Death and Dying.*[xxii] Throughout the 70s and 80s, management consulting firms developed and they quickly found that organizational behavior and employees in organizations followed a similar grief pattern from the time of announcement of change through some acceptable level of new commitment. This model has been around forever and is somewhat less than fully interesting. What is more interesting is how leaders interact with groups of humans going through transformation, and how they bring them to some level of acceptable commitment as quickly as possible. While one can never compress the model vertically, a leader can move groups through the model horizontally more quickly or less quickly, depending on his or her behaviors, attitudes, and language.

The Zone of Transformation

The disciplined leader is aware of the typical process humans go through when they experience change. First, they enter the zone of transformation. We enter the zone of transformation when something else is ending. This is how we know we're in a significant change event. We're moving along our professional life, or our lives in general, and then something changes. That something usually is marked by the end of the status quo—the technology system, the name on our paycheck, or the way we interact with our work. Changes come in all forms, from promotion to job loss to a new location. When we enter the zone of transformation we go from what is the known in the world to what is unknown. It turns out humans do not like to not know. So, during the zone of transformation, humans will use rumors to make up information rather than knowing nothing. Humans will become anxious in many cases and therefore unable to be fully productive. And distractions become noise. A leader who understands what typically happens to most people in the zone of transformation has an advantage. That advantage comes from understanding this is a normal process and should not be a blaming process. When leaders begin to use the word "they," they separate themselves from the normal human condition and therefore lose effectiveness. When a leader understands all humans experience change as a crisis and an opportunity, and entering the zone of transformation brings predictable grieving steps, one can lead much more effectively and with more discipline and more intention.

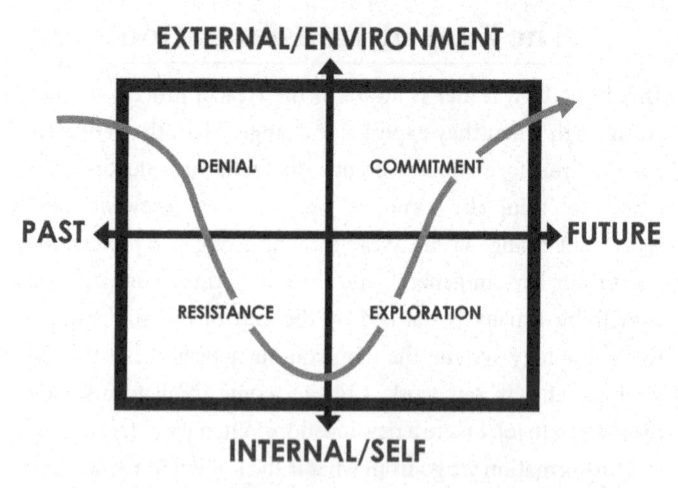

Figure 14. The Grief Curve (Based on a Model Originally Developed by Elisabeth Kübler-Ross)[xxiii]

Specifically, as one enters the zone of transformation, we can predict that people will experience disbelief or even shock. This is why we communicate with urgency and balance rather than happiness or glibness. We repeat and we move rapidly through a series of communications at the smallest level. We put in change champions and teams to create a two-way dialogue rather than a one-way push via email or all hands meetings. Immediately putting in a two-way communication mechanism driven by team leaders demonstrates that change leadership requires more than a single person to generate a critical mass of engagement and productivity as quickly as possible. These two-way mechanisms need to happen immediately at the time an announcement is pushed out, with as much information as we have. We need to seek points of concern and generally get input or incoming information as quickly as possible. This incoming information allows us to head off points of crisis, as well as to build a better change plan.

One of the greatest change tools one can have is simply talking to your constituents like this: "I can speak to you about what I know, I can openly speak to you about what I don't know, and I would love to hear your questions or concerns." As an individual leader, using that tool as a communication technique when people are anxious is very effective. So, in this first phase of the zone of transformation, one needs to put in place two-way communication mechanisms, immediately pushing out as much as we can and remembering to treat adults like adults. My advice is this: I have watched many leaders treat grown adults like children in times of change and instantly lose credibility.

Before moving to the second part of the zone of transformation, which is resistance, it's important to mention that having a project plan is not enough. Developing a change plan using John Kotter's eight-step model as the outline can be very helpful.[xxiv] For example, in times of change, we start with an urgent statement. We build guiding teams and then we create the vision of a better future. While this order may seem simplistic, it's critical to gaining credibility and buy-in quickly. We typically see these three steps being taken at the time of announcement through to the time of predicted resistance, which would be day one after announcement.

Resistance to Change

Now let's discuss resistance. People themselves are not resistant, and resistance in itself is not negative resistance, it's a part of the human condition. We need to plan for resistance, and in fact use it to build a better strategic change plan. As a part of our plan, our goal is never to get all employees to the other side of the change. Rather, it's to develop a critical mass of early adopters, influencers—or as Gladwell calls them, mavens and resistors.[xxv] We want to develop small groups of critical employees who would fit these descriptors. We want to put them together and begin the two-way dialogue process. As a part of the two-way dialogue process, we want to actively seek the points of resistance. In times of status quo, we can sometimes walk by resistance or not deal with it because it's too burdensome. But in times of change, we want to actively seek resistance.

Here's how it really works. Most resistance in organizations is passive. Our goal is to take passive resistance and make it active. Think about it this way: We want the watercooler chatter to be sanctioned and bring it into the small steering team meeting. We want to create psychological safety for resistance discipline leaders. We know the more we can formalize the expression of resistance, the better problem identification we have and the more steam we can blow out of the pressure. Allowing people to express resistance without going negative is a discipline, and it's critical to allow people to move through the zone of transformation.

As we seek to make resistance active, we can then enroll and engage them in the how. We can allow resistors to identify new success criteria and metrics we can use, and allow resistors to take on key leadership roles to actually get their hands dirty during the change. One of the things the wise change leader does is to get as much involvement on the actual change tasks as possible. We need early adopters right next to influencers and resistors, as they work on the change itself, as well as enroll them in leading change activities like running focus groups and creating metrics for success in delivering results to the workforce. The change leader understands and creates forums for this, identifying the stakeholders in a very deliberate and intentional way.

Exploring Transformation

As we move from resistance to exploration, the task becomes to realign how people engage with their work, to re-define incentives, and to allow early successes to be celebrated. This is how we make the change stick and allow people to explore and commit. Being a change leader is to understand that all change involves crisis and opportunity. The typical human response to change is to enter the change curve via the zone of transformation. Our role is to embrace the typical human response to change and accelerate groups of people moving through it toward the fastest engagement and productivity possible. If we can't define what engagement and productivity look like, how will large groups of followers?

Here are the key concepts to keep in mind during transformation:

- Zone of transformation
- Producing lasting change and transition
- Coaching during the phases of transition
- The tools for change (Toolkit Review)

This figure describes several tools that can go into your change toolbox. I was raised by electricians. In all of my uncles' and aunts' houses, there was a scary-looking tool that was called a voltage tester. When I inquired about what this thing was, I was told that it allowed us to see if there was hot electricity in an outlet. This tool was critical to my uncle's survival. It's similar to the way people who struggle with change often don't have the understanding of typical human behavior, the right mindset, and finally a well-worn set of proven tools.

Of course, if you're going through a large-scale change, you want a communications plan. You might want to map out the

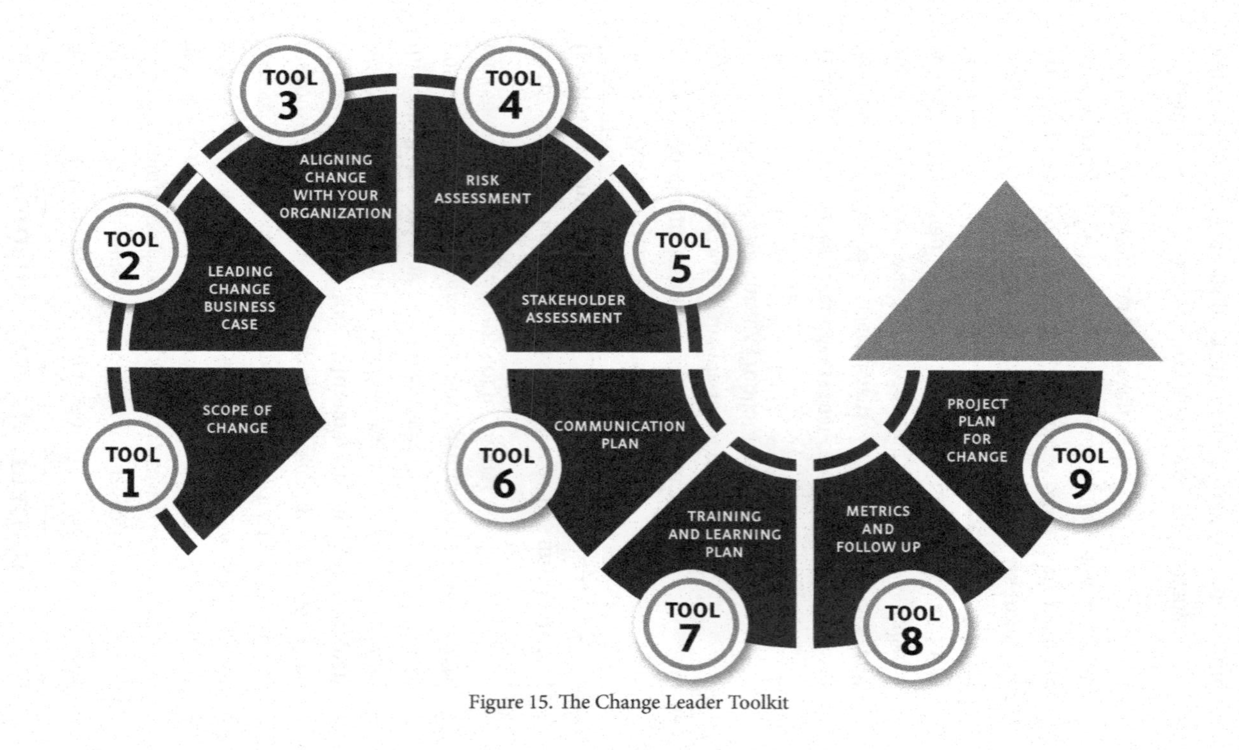

Figure 15. The Change Leader Toolkit

stakeholders who will have to own the change, understand the change, or simply have awareness of the change. A stakeholder map helps you with that. Remember, we don't need everyone on board. We need the owners on board and the people who have to understand the change to be mapped and addressed accordingly. Another example is a risk assessment. Imagine you're in the elevator as you lead a large change and your chairman or CEO asks you about one of the largest risks you're concerned about. Well, if you and your steering team have done several risk assessments, you can clearly articulate the top 3 to 5 risks, along with mitigating strategies. This might seem like common sense, but you can see that it's the use of a tool that will help you drive the change. The tools referenced on the above page are easily accessed with a simple google search,

In summary, the disciplined leader treats a time of change differently and leads differently in this time of change. It is no longer about efficiency and vision. It is now about understanding that groups of humans experience anxiety and change in regular and predictable ways. It's understanding how to move people through the zone of transformation. And finally, it's understanding what's needed to get into engagement and productivity as fast as possible. Being a change leader requires the mindset that all change is both crisis and opportunity, and the opportunity to be viewed as a highly effective leader doesn't come in everyday life. It comes from our transitions.

PROCESS	CONTENT
How comfortable are you with change	A mindset
How have you been negatively and positively affected by change	Types of change
Do you seek discomfort	The typical response to change
Are you as comfortable working with resistors as early adopters	Developing a change plan to lead from

Even when change is thrust upon us, we as leaders need to react quickly and lead people through the change. This chapter speaks of the mindset to lead change, the typical human response to change, and the specific leader behaviors and tools that can be deployed to lead groups of people through significant change. A dynamic leader and a dynamic organization understands that in industry and our environment, people are actually driving continuous improvement constantly. A leader's ability to meet humans and help them through change is absolutely critical. Having the best idea and the best action plan is interesting, but our focus should be getting engagement, performance, and productivity out of individuals and teams.

CHAPTER 8

The Discipline of Building Executive Presence

WE'VE WALKED THROUGH the disciplines of introspection and self-awareness, the discipline of creating an environment, the discipline of influencing without power, and the discipline to become a great coach, and in Chapter 5, the discipline to build great teams and to truly understand group dynamics. As we leave job or occupational mastery and journey toward being a great leader, we find that we actually begin to think differently. We have built specific strategic thinking muscles. Finally, we are constantly working on our executive presence. It is an act of trimming the sails. We are never perfect, but we are seeking to be the adult in the room.

Executive presence adds an element of maturity when it comes to providing leadership. It is worth noting that the term "executive presence" has been loosely defined, and even less well understood in the past. Oftentimes executive presence has been coded language to potentially keep women and people of color out of key leadership positions. If you look up some literature on executive presence, there either isn't anything satisfactory, or what is out there is loose and scattered. Having said that, there is a real discipline in having true senior leadership presence. While it may be hard to define, it's easily observable. In this chapter we will offer the 3D Model and break it down into core elements that describe the discipline of having executive presence.

The 3D Model

To help my clients better understand executive presence and how to build it, I have developed the 3D Model. The 3D Model consists of Define, Declare, and Demonstrate. The 3D Model will enable you to break down executive presence into its elements.

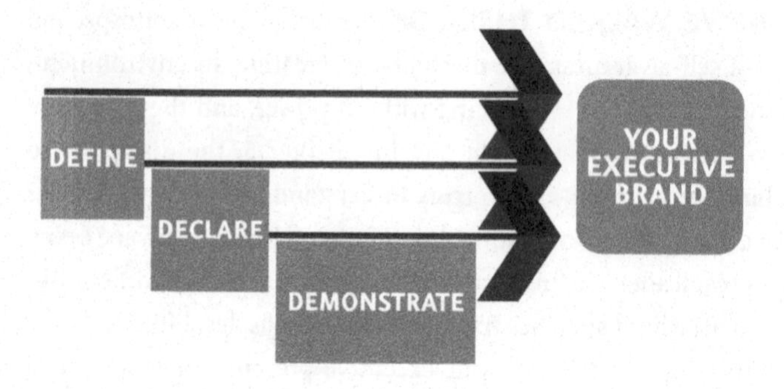

Figure 16. The 3D Model

The Define phase is where a leader seeks to deeply understand herself and define her core values, vision, stressors, motivators, and a variety of other strengths and weaknesses that one can derive from emotional intelligence assessments, personality assessments, and other forms of leadership assessment. This is where we define all of the elements of who we are as a leader. We can refer back to Chapter 1, where we talk about introspection and the power of emotional intelligence as we seek to increase our leadership effectiveness. One who has not gone through the process of accurately and rigorously defining themselves would have a hard time demonstrating steadiness and being the adult in the room. How can one be comfortable in one's own skin if one doesn't know what is inside that skin?

In the Declare phase, we can harken back to the LBI framework, which is a framework for influencing other human beings. In the Declare phase, one demonstrates comfort in discussing principles, direction, strategy, and vision. The Declare phase is where the leader becomes known to others.

The 3D Model can be traced back to branding. In any good branding campaign where we want to define the elements of our product or service, we message the attributes in a way that influences behavior, and then we follow through on that declaration with our demonstrated behaviors. In executive presence, we think about a very similar track. In the Declaration Phase, we are putting forth the brand promise of what a follower or an employee or anyone who would be influenced by this executive leader will understand. Am I assertive, am I passive, am I thoughtful? Am I reactive in the way that I behave and the language that I use and am I in control of how others experience me? The accuracy in which I define and declare myself allows others to follow me. Without good declarative content, we can unwittingly make it difficult for people to be influenced by us or follow us. Is my messaging concise, consistent, and clear? The extent that my declaration of my leadership strengths and weaknesses and the direction I would like to go are clear or unclear would likely be the extent to which I could engender followership. Think about the Declare phase as "how I will be known to others through my use of language and my modeling of behaviors."

More precisely, it's in the Demonstrate phase where the modeling of behaviors is a primary activity. Like any brand, we must follow through on the brand promise. As a leader, am I demonstrating courage and humility, innovation, risk, and steadiness in times of crisis? Ralph Waldo Emerson once said, "Man cannot be great in his everyday pursuits. Man can be great in his transitions." How do you show up when others would be rattled? The demonstration of steadiness, emotional maturity, caring, and strategic thinking are critical content components of our behavior. The demonstration of leadership steadiness gives consumers of your leadership the perception of your executive presence.

A note on bias: In our culture, there is a bias toward a tall white male as the archetype of a leader. While that may be a controversial statement, the data is quite clear that women and people of color don't show up in senior leadership positions at the same rate as white men. However, being a white male is not a prerequisite for executive presence. It does turn out that the assignment of good executive presence is culturally constrained and has some element of implicit bias in it. However, my premise is that executive presence can be developed as a discipline for any aspiring leader through the process of their development.

So let's start with the process. Have you gone through the process to develop a clear definition of who you are, developed concise messaging about what you intend to do as a leader, and demonstrated emotional intelligence and maturity to show up when others are in need of leadership? The process of going through crucibles in one's leadership life is the process of learning through challenges and failure.

The content for executive presence, while all over the place in the literature, appears to be fairly clear to me. The demonstration of the attributes of emotional intelligence, strategic, clear and objective decision-making, appropriate risk taking, and vulnerability appear to be the content required at a minimum to be assigned healthy and good executive presence.

So as we seek to develop the discipline of executive presence, we can start with the 3D Model and then rigorously walk ourselves through the 3Ds again and again. We look for the process of events to train our body and our behaviors to show up when it matters most in a steady way, such that others can and are willing to follow us. And from a content perspective, do we know what the attributes of presence are?

The Steps to Developing Executive Presence

So where does one start? Step One, to build the discipline of executive presence, has been explained above. There is a very strong correlation between high emotional intelligence and senior leadership effectiveness. If one wants to develop the discipline of executive presence, one then starts with increasing and developing attributes of emotional intelligence. We can see elements of the 3D Model in the core elements of emotional intelligence. Self-awareness would speak to the Define Phase. Self-regulation and self-motivation would speak to the Declare and Demonstrate Phase, as would empathy and relationship building. If one was to work on those core elements of emotional intelligence, one will inherently developed great presence.

Step Two in developing executive presence is to be very clear in your definition, declaration, and demonstration of your core values and your vision. Having solid core values and vision at a minimum enables others to understand you, and therefore, be able to follow you. You are not whimsical; you're steady and consistent. In a world that might need to pull you in many different directions, you are always able to come back and either challenge or reinforce your existing values and vision.

Step Three is actively and intentionally driving not followership, but engagement of all the stakeholders in your leadership ecosystem. Let me explain. A leader who actively seeks to drive engagement of others will get more done than a leader who is ignorant around what engagement is. Engagement has been studied in organizational behavior. It is constructed of:

1. A solid relationship with your boss,
2. solid relationships with other team members and peers,
3. the meaningfulness of one's work, and
4. fair and equitable incentives.

A leader who intentionally drives engagement in other people and seeks to increase engagement would likely get more productivity and satisfaction from those people. So having executive presence therefore would be the act of building relationships with others, enabling relationships between people and subgroups, providing meaningfulness of work through values and vision, and actively incenting a fair and equitable workplace. A leader who seeks engagement can expect to get discretionary effort from people. Engagement therefore is different than followership in that engagement seeks to drive the discretionary psychological, emotional, and physical effort from people in our ecosystem.

Step Four in building one's executive presence would literally be the ability to present oneself and present materials in a highly effective way in all circumstances. Whether walking down the hallway or presenting in front of a group of 50 senior leaders, one should be crystal clear of one's purpose and audience and choose the right structure for the interaction.

We should never be surprised. Lay people might understand this as being a highly effective communicator, but it is so much more. For example, in a moment when I'm presented with a customer in a hallway walking with one of my sales reps, I instantly go through what is my purpose for this interaction, who might this person be, what might they need from me, and how should I structure the interaction. When I go through that in less than a split second, I can now be deliberate and intentional as a leader and leave the impression that I intend to leave. To take that example out further, it would be to develop a warm relationship, not to sell the person anything that would be overeager and junior. I would want to have a short interaction and I would want the person to want to learn more about me and our business as I walked away. So as I think about the purpose, the audience and the structure for that 30-second interaction, I would be able to form an interaction with some level of intentionality. To have executive presence is to not be whimsical. It is to be deliberate and intentional as the adult in the room, or the leader in all cases. A way to think about that is to think about the purpose, audience, and structure for all interactions.

Challenge, Action, Result

I have been offered the positive complement of having executive presence and I'm convinced that the idea of purpose, audience, and structure has gotten me fairly far along this road. More specifically, I like the CAR acronym. When interacting in a team meeting or interacting in an informal conversation, I typically will try to leverage the CAR framework. The C is the

Challenge—what is the business challenge or business question? A is for Action. What is the desired action, previous action, or the current actions I am undertaking to move forward on the business challenge or question? And then I end with the R, the result. What is the desired result or outcome, or what result did we get that may want to revisit.

The CAR Model allows for conciseness, clarity, and consistency, whether being asked a question or presenting information. This is just one example of structuring my interactions so that I can increase my influence, not be whimsical, and present myself in a business-focused leadership way. There are many other communication frameworks that can be just as helpful, but to develop executive presence means to be emotionally intelligent, to use the 3D Model to unpack elements of yourself, to be rooted in values and vision, and finally to have a purpose with any audience, and have a structure when interacting with other humans.

Now, if this all sounds difficult, it may be, but it is tested under times of stress and tension. Anyone can have executive presence in any status quo moment. The disciplined leader is able to have executive presence when stress is increased and others need leadership. The process of developing that presence requires repetition in awkwardness, in stress, and even in discomfort. From a process standpoint, to seek out those crucible moments to practice one's presence is a key developmental technique to develop greater presence.

Chapter 9

Final Thoughts

WE STARTED THIS JOURNEY by asking why I wrote this book, and why you should read it.

I am ever wonderous of how in almost all cases human beings know the right thing to do, but often do not choose the right thing to do. This book, like many others, is screaming: "Hey person that is not deliberately and intentionally leading, you are negatively impacting other human beings." There are fact-based things leaders must do to have a more positive impact on other human beings. We spend so much time working, why not endeavor to PRACTICE your leadership effectiveness every day while working.

We know most of the content and processes to increase leadership effectiveness, but for many, we simply don't choose the practice or discipline. **Discipline means to teach.** In the text of this book, we assert 8 Disciplines to increase one's leadership effectiveness. Those disciplines are best practiced and learned through the content (what) and process (how and why) of leading. To be clear, there are many other things to learn about when it comes to leading in organizations, the military, the community, etc. This book was by no means intended to be the end-all be-all of leadership. There is no perfect leader and there is no ONE definitive place, or book, or TED talk to become the perfect leader. In fact, perfection as a leader is a myth. Increasing one's leadership effectiveness through daily practice and discipline is the key to the journey toward greater leadership effectiveness. This book may be just one step on that journey for the reader.

This book seeks to not only serve as an 8-step journey toward greater leadership effectiveness, it also explores the basis for poor leadership. When we can unbundle **both** the process and the content for becoming an effective leader, our work becomes a bit more clear. The ideas outlined in this book are fundamental disciplines, which leaders across all types of organizations can leverage to ascend in their careers, achieve great enterprise leadership, and harness the power of discomfort to accelerate their growth.

The truth is, becoming a great leader is not that simple. Authentic leadership development requires **rigor**, a great deal of **discipline** and **practice**, and above all, **deliberate** and **intentional** attitudes, beliefs, and behaviors. Great leadership should lead to great enjoyment, satisfaction, and reward for the people you serve as a leader. This is the critical reason "why" you need to go through 8 Disciplines.

Endeavoring to have a positive impact on people whom you know, serve, and partner with every day requires one to be on a never-ending journey toward greater leadership effectiveness. We all have a leader or two for whom we would do almost anything. Those leaders had a great impact on us. The truth is, if you ask yourself why that leader is so effective, you will almost always land on attributes associated with the 8 Disciplines below:

1. The Discipline of Introspection and "Intro-Action" (YOU)
2. The Discipline of Finding Your Voice and Developing Your Culture and Vision (Projecting YOU)
3. The Discipline of Influencing With or Without Charisma
4. The Discipline of ENABLING Productivity and Performance (Leading in an Organization)
5. The Discipline of Building GREAT Teams and Groups (Leading in an Organization)
6. The Discipline of Strategic Thinking
7. The Discipline of Being a Change Leader
8. The Discipline of Building Executive Presence

The attributes likely include caring, authenticity, self-awareness, trust, strategic thinking, continuously improving, coaching, great teams, vision, and enthusiasm. Through the process of rigorous development, I know that all of us can develop toward greater leadership effectiveness and a greater impact on our fellow human beings.

Acknowledgments

PEOPLE OFTEN DEBATE: are leaders born or can they be made? The answer to me is obvious—both! In any given culture there are certain advantages or disadvantages one possesses relative to one's physical characteristics. It's not popular to talk about but true. These physical characteristics are nothing more than a starting point for one's leadership journey and by no means do they define leadership effectiveness.

Of course, we know now that while those physical characteristics are only a starting point, great leaders are in fact MOSTLY "made." Most critical for highly effective leaders is the "made" part. One starts the "made" part of one's leadership development journey at birth, influenced heavily by family of origin, nutrition, community, education, and employment experiences, not to mention military or athletic exposure. While this paragraph could easily become a book on its own, I only touch on this as I reflect on the nature of acknowledging those in my life who have been instrumental in supporting and contributing to my growth as a leader.

I am, and have been, more heavily influenced by my family origin than I even realize today. It is easy to point to a coach, teacher or mentor as a person who greatly influenced me because I was partially awake when they influenced me. I was a teenager and young adult when those people influenced me. In fact, for better and for worse I—and many others—were and are heavily influenced toward leadership by our / my family of origin.

My mother and father brought me into the world when they were much too young—not uncommon for people of my generation. While I suspect my upbringing was not too dissimilar from other lower middle-income people from the east coast being raised in the 1970s and 80s, Michael and Sandy Brainard's struggle, love for me and my brother (Matt) and sister (Shannon), and choices, MOSTLY shaped my leadership style and philosophy. Their support for me when it was not easy to support me caused me to want to lead, and further want to study this thing called leadership. My parents led me, inspired me to lead, and stoked my curiosity. Michael and Sandy are the primary drivers of my leadership journey. This journey will never end as I am imperfect and there is no perfect leader. Michael and Sandy instilled in me perseverance, grit, and curiosity. This book is primarily dedicated to my parents as they were primarily dedicated to me, Matt, and Shannon.

I was supported by a broader family of origin—again, not dissimilar from others. I was supported by loving grandparents, uncles and aunts, cousins, and a community. While never perfect, I shudder to think about children not supported by a broader family of origin and community. So many children do not have these advantages, and while their struggle may be more challenging than others, their struggle facilitates a different leadership journey. My leadership journey was no doubt made better by these influences, most specifically my Grandfather (pop pop): Jack Brainard. Jack was a WWII Marine, union electrician, father of seven children, and provider for his family.

His core values seeped through his pores and his love for me gave me ambition and steadiness, as well as courage.

Part of my community was always coaches and teachers. The Colonial School District and Salesianum High School shaped me. Much of my drive and searching has come from many teachers and coaches from the above-mentioned institutions. People in my home state of Delaware will chuckle when I say two rival high school coaches, John Rusnak and Jack Holloway, are due a debt of gratitude for inspiring me. Uncle John Rusnak, Timothy Szymansky and the Szymansky family, Jim Brazil, George Glenn, Brian Donahue, Jon Meys, Jeff Braxton, Mike Pinkett, Carl Bond, Paul Schweizer, Vaughn Bolton, Dr. Michael Axe, Dr. Cooper, Paul Billy and Dr. Tim Scott; and many more (too many to mention) have all shaped both me as a leader and my curiosity about highly effective leaders and leadership. My parents sacrificed greatly for my participation in many sports, but wrestling likely taught me more than anything else the value of discipline, sacrifice and accountability. Even more critically, my parents sacrificed so that I could attend Salesianum High School. Sallies holds a very special place in my life because without the academic rigor, commitment to excellence, and the peer group it afforded me, I can promise that neither this book nor my life as I know it would be as it is today.

My clients over the past 25 years have taught me while thinking I was helping them. Each and every experience that my clients have entrusted me with has become a critical element in my leadership practice and research. From the small engagements to the largest and most complex, this book would NOT be possible without those clients. Early in my career I thought I wanted to research. Once I experienced change in my clients, I caught fire. My clients have led me, taught me, supported me, and inspired me. I have come to love the PRACTICE of developing leaders and facilitating growth and development of leaders, teams, and organizations. Without my clients I would not be able to have the confidence to write my thoughts down in the form of this book. I am indebted to my client partners.

Over the years I have been fortunate to work with many talented and bright colleagues. Jim Greenway, Sandra Smith, Ken Ruggiero, Kevin Francis, Bob Hurley, Morgan O'Brien, Bob Gilbert, Maggie Osburn, Tom Triolo, Jack Farnan, Jonathan Schoonmaker, Scott Paine, Dale Harris, Elijah Seay, and Claudia Kennedy each have shaped me as a person and as a leader. I have learned the value of balancing humility and confidence, optimism and pessimism, and my impact on other human beings through the above mentioned, and many other people with whom I have called colleagues.

Thank you to my friends who have provided continuous learning over the years: Rob Mackle, Greg Welch, Paul Vaden, Jay Zayer, Scott Golueke, Kent Buckson, Todd Fritchman, Brent Rivard, Eric Roden, and Greg Pullman.

My family is a unique blend of love, challenge and an infinite searching to be better. Kelly Kambs is my wife, a corporate executive, a mom to now four children, and the source of something I never experienced before in my life outside of a family member—unconditional love. Kelly is smart, most kind, and a source of infinite love. I am certainly not capable of loving like Kelly. It is almost like a superpower. I have learned more form Kelly in the past seven years than any single person I have ever encountered. Many evenings I will come home from the airport or work, and I will walk into a room of 10 "strangers." Turns out Kelly doesn't understand the word "stranger." One night I could walk into a room filled with her colleagues from 20 years ago who are in town and had to look her up. On another night, I walk into a room with moms that she met at a swim meet, and on another night, she might be entertaining some extended family members or neighbors. Kelly has taught me the value of love, connection, and the unconditional acceptance of oneself and others for who they are. Kelly has made me a better person and a more thoughtful leader.

My ex-wife Dr. Richene Bevilaqua and I work (with many others) to raise Mykelle Brainard. Richene has been gracious with me when I did not deserve that graciousness, and now, we parent this AMAZING and INSPIRATIONAL human being named Mykelle (Elle). Everyone brags about their child, so I won't bore you, BUT... I truly get inspiration from watching Elle each and every day. Her unyielding positivity, work ethic, involvement, and engagement in her community are light years beyond what I am capable of now as an adult, let alone when I was 17.

About Michael Brainard

AS THE CEO and Founder of Brainard Strategy, Michael Brainard has amassed over 20 years of experience as a management consultant, C-level senior executive, executive coach, entrepreneur, and researcher. Through his management consulting work, Michael has designed and implemented systems re-engineering, organizational assessments, leadership development initiatives, and performance management systems. Michael also draws additional experience from his work as an internal and external post-acquisition integration leader.

Michael's extensive educational background (MA, MS, Ph.D.) has afforded him a unique understanding of psychological principles that he leverages to help facilitate growth in other like-minded business leaders. As a keynote speaker, Michael has delivered addresses to such groups as the Association for Corporate Growth, TEDx, PIHRA, SHRM, PCMA, OCEMA, and NHRA. Michael's most requested presentation is on unconscious bias and, more specifically, the Bias Trifecta—his unique illustration of Unconscious Bias, Retroactive Inference, and Confirmation Bias—and how it impacts leadership decision-making.

A former professional boxer, Brainard holds a bachelor's degree in psychology from the University of Delaware, where he was a Division I collegiate wrestler. Additionally, he earned both his master's degree and Ph.D. in industrial psychology at Alliant International University in San Diego, California.

As a doctor of industrial and organizational psychology, an entrepreneur and former senior corporate executive in both publicly traded consulting firms and financial services firms, Brainard possesses a unique perspective and understanding of the subtle psychological principles of leadership and organizational development. Through his confidential work with executives, he has become renowned for his ability to motivate and energize leaders from diverse backgrounds, as well as identify potential areas of opportunity, while facilitating growth. Past and present clients include the likes of: Beckman Coulter, Memorial Healthcare, Sequenom, Golden State Foods, Celanese, VMWare, Allergan, Experian, Goal Financial, Howard Building Corporaation, National Semiconductor, Glidewell Dental, Invitrogen, Lyon Living, Conagra, Dell, Scripps, Baker Engineering, Qualcomm, and Ericsson, among others.

With an approach that blends strategic, behavioral and experiential learning, Michael has successfully developed growth strategies for executives and businesses in a wide range of industries including biotechnology, manufacturing, information services, consumer packaged goods, financial services, telecommunications and construction.

Finally, in his capacity as a researcher, Michael has contributed to myriad publications with his empirical findings on performance appraisal systems, telecommuting, and leadership development. Brainard is also a member of the Forbes Coaches Council, where he regularly contributes fresh content on a wide array of subject matter, such as "*A Framework for Succeeding as a First Time CEO,*" "*Effects of Social Isolation as a Result of the Pandemic,*" and "*Busting the Myth of Perfection in Business.*"

Michael's specialties include: Organizational Assessment, Strategic Planning, Strategic Alignment & Implementation, Board Assessment, Business Process Consultation, Mergers & Acquisitions Integration, Organizational Design & Structure, Re-structure & Downsizing, Change Management, Executive Coaching, Leadership Development, Culture & Climate Survey, Team Building & Executive Alignment, Talent Acquisition & Talent Management, Performance Management, Total Rewards & Compensation.

For more information, or to contact Michael directly, you can find him on LinkedIn.

Additional Reading

Bossidy, Larry, and Ram Charan, Charles Burck. *Execution: The Discipline of Getting Things Done*. Random House, 2011.

Bradberry,Travis, and Jean Greaves. *Emotional Intelligence 2.0*. TalentSmart, 2009.

Carter, Louis, and David Giber, Marshall Goldsmith. *Best Practices in Leadership Development Handbook*. Jossey-Bass/ Pfeiffer and Linkage Inc., 2000.

Collins, James C., and Jerry I. Porras. *Built to Last: Successful Habits of Visionary Companies*. Harvard Business Essentials, 2002.

Covey, Stephen R. *The 7 Habits of Highly Effective People*. Franklin Covey, 1998.

Crane, Thomas G., and Lerissa Nancy Patrick. *The Heart of Coaching: Using Transformational Coaching to Create a High-Performance Coaching Culture*. FTA Press, 2014.

Eblin, Scott. *The Next Level: What Insiders Know about Executive Success*. Nicholas Brealey Publishing, 2018.

George, Bill. *Authentic Leadership: Rediscovering the Secrets to Creating Lasting Value*. Jossey-Bass, 2004.

Hargrove, Robert. *Masterful Coaching*. Wiley, 2008.

Jansen, Kraemer Harry M. *From Values to Action: The Four Principles of Values-Based Leadership*. Jossey-Bass, 2011.

Kouzes, James M., and Barry Z. Posner. *The Leadership Challenge*. Jossey-Bass, 2003.

Lombardo, Michael M., and Robert W. Eichinger. *Career Architect Development Planner*. Lominger International, 2004.

Lombardo, Michael J., and Robert W. Eichinger. *For Your Improvement: A Guide for Development and Coaching for Learners, Managers, Mentors, and Feedback Givers*. Lominger International, 2006.

Senor, Dan, and Saul Singer. *Start-up Nation: The Story of Israel's Economic Miracle*. Twelve, 2011.

Stone, Douglas, and Sheila Heen. *Thanks for the Feedback: The Science and Art of Receiving Feedback Well: (even when it is off base, unfair, poorly delivered, and, frankly, you're not in the mood)*. Portfolio Penguin, 2019.

Endnotes

Chapter 1

i Goleman, Daniel. *Emotional Intelligence*. New York: Toronto, 1995.

ii Salovey, Peter and John D. Mayer. "Emotional Intelligence", published in *Imagination, Cognition and Personality*. Volume 9, Issue 3. March 1, 1990.

iii Goleman, Daniel.

iv Helmholtz, Hermann von. *Handbuch der Physiologischen Optik*. Leipzig, 1867.

v Simmons, Daniel. "Seeing the world as it isn't" TED Talk, March 19, 2011. https://www.youtube.com/watch?v=9Il_D3Xt9W0.

vi Collins, James C. *Good to Great*. Random House Business, 2001.

vii The Arbinger Institute. *Leadership and Self-Deception: Getting Out of the Box*. Berrett-Koehler Publishers, 2018.

viii The Arbinger Institute.

ix Collins, James C.

Chapter 3

x Schein, Edgar H. *Organizational Culture and Leadership*. Jossey-Bass, 2010.

xi Nanus, Burt. *Visionary Leadership: Creating a Compelling Sense of Direction for Your Organization*. Jossey-Bass, 1995.

xii Egon Zehnder International and McKinsey & Company. Joint study "Return on Leadership – Competencies that Generate Growth", February 2011.

xiii Sinek, Simon. "How great leaders inspire action" TED Talk, May 4, 2010. https://www.youtube.com/watch?v=qp0HIF3SfI4.

Chapter 5

[xiv] Lewicki, R. J., Barry, B. & Saunders, D. M. *Essentials of Negotiation* (4th Edition). Mc-Graw-Hill/Irwin. 2004. Print

[xv] Bracey, Hyler. *Building Trust: How to Get it! How to Keep it!* Hyler Bracey, 2010

[xvi] Hackman, J. Richard and Ruth Wageman. "A Theory of Team Coaching", published in Academy of Management Review. Volume 30, Issue 2. April 1, 2005.

[xvii] Lencioni, Patrick. *The Five Dysfunctions of a Team: Facilitator's Guide: The Official Guide to Conducting the Five Dysfunctions Workshops for Teams and Team Leaders*. Chichester, 2012.

[xviii] Lencioni, Patrick.

Chapter 7

[xix] Collins, James C. *Level 5 Leadership: The Triumph of Humility and Fierce Resolve*. Boston: Harvard Business School Pub., 2001.

[xx] Peters, Thomas J., and Robert H. Waterman. *In Search of Excellence: Lessons from America's Best-Run Compagnies*. New York etc.: Harper & Row, 1984.

[xxi] Dweck, Carol S. *Mindset*. London: Robinson, 2017.

[xxii] Kübler-Ross Elisabeth. *On Death and Dying ; Questions and Answers on Death and Dying ; on Life after Death*. New York: Quality Paperback Book Club, 2002.

[xxiii] Kübler-Ross Elisabeth.

[xxiv] Kotter, John P. *Leading Change*. Harvard Business Review Press, 2012.

[xxv] Gladwell, Malcolm. *Blink: The Power of Thinking Without Thinking*. Back Bay Books, 2019.

5 hybrid (virtual or in person) instructor-led modules, assessments, networking with leaders from various industries and executive coaching

brainard
STRATEGY

Brainard Strategy exceeded our expectations assisting us in implementing our first executive leadership development program. The Executives who participated in EXCELerateSM grew significantly as leaders through this robust and vigorous development program. They actively engaged with one another to form new and deeper relationships. Brainard Strategy's EXCELerateSM program has been a catalyst for change in our organization. We have already seen the impact it has had on our executives' direct reports and are excited to watch the impact continue long after the program concludes.

Jeff Filley, President
Behr Paint

Michael Brainard's direct approach and willingness to directly challenge high performing individuals is refreshing. The entire EXCELerate team is excellent – always willing to assist. Most importantly Michael's use of Psychology intermixed with Best in Breed Leadership concepts creates a framework to not only grow during the program but to take those learnings into the months and years ahead – enabling the graduate to continually develop as an Executive Leader.

Richard DeVos
Controller

To learn more about our Stevie Award-winning executive development program, EXCELerate, **navigate to https://www.brainardstrategy.com/excelerate/** or email: **info@brainardstrategy.com**

The program is offered twice per year, in April and September. See you then!